About this Book

Taming a language gone mad

To the uninitiated, a Jazz concert may sound cacophonous and undisciplined, when in fact it has its roots in structured classical music forms. And so it is with English, especially American English. Drawn from a multitude of sources, dragged across the Atlantic and further modified, it too seems to lack any sense of consistency. Though we have no formal system for codifying and regulating the language, there is a root system (accepted by scholars) onto which is grafted the never-ending changes (frequently decried by scholars) which characterize the language.

Written in an easy to understand, relaxed style, with handy references to assist the user, here is a (sometimes irreverent) handbook for anyone who seeks a better understanding of American English and how to use it most effectively.

WEBSTER'S GRAMMAR HANDBOOK

WEBSTER'S GRAMMAR HANDBOOK

Pamco Publishing Company, Inc.

ISBN: 1-881275-16-7

TABLE OF CONTENTS

Part III - Basic Grammar — Putting It All Together

Part I

Background of American English

Background of American English

Do you wonder why English spelling is so difficult? Why we don't just spell things the way they sound? Or say things the way they are spelled? Why different groups of letters all sound the same? Or why one group of letters gets pronounced in so many ways? How could anyone have come up with such a system?

Well, it wasn't done by just anyone, and certainly not by design. English was formed from a merging of primitive dialects which were then shaped and embellished by others. English didn't happen all at once in one place, but in isolated pockets of independent peoples who didn't have a common language even after they united to form a nation. And the changes continue . . . .

ENGLISH — A BRIEF HISTORY

If we want to understand today's English and its irregularities, we need to look at how it was formed and shaped over the past fifteen hundred years. We may then come to understand how futile were the attempts to regularize such things as spelling and pronunciation. We may even come to agree that English is far richer for never having had tight reins placed on it.

Exit Romans, enter Barbarians

Picture this. It's the middle of the fifth century. On an island called Britain, the native Celts have been ruled by the Romans for almost four hundred years. The Roman Empire runs into trouble and the troops are called home. As the Celts watch the Romans leave, they in turn are being watched by the Germanic peoples of northern Europe who see a fine land, ripe for settlement. As far as we know, the tribes which settle in Britain are not invading in force, but are part of a migration which lasts several generations. They gradually displace those Celts who survive their incursions. Apparently few Celts remain in the areas occupied by the tribes, for there is little trace of the Celtic tongue in the language that evolves. Ultimately pockets of Angles, Saxons,

Jutes, and Friscians are scattered throughout the whole of Britain except for Scotland and Wales, which remain in Celtic hands.

Consider the change which has taken place. The way of the Romans is to conquer, then inform the survivors that they are a part of the Roman Empire for which privilege they will be allowed to work their land and pay taxes to Rome. The Romans, proud of their own language and culture, are content to rule and remain largely indifferent to the customs and culture of the peoples they rule. The Celts, for their part, live a relatively civilized and orderly existence under the Romans. The Germanic tribes which fill the vacuum left by the departure of the Romans have no proud history and grand cause for which they fight; they simply want the land and view anyone occupying it as an inconvenience. There is no common language and the Germanic dialects, each altered by contact with others through trade or war, may be similar, but are not the same.

The Angles and Saxons

The new occupants of Britain have no central government and little contact with each other. Most tend to their own land and never leave the village where they are born, a way of life which persists for centuries. There is, however, change. Perhaps it begins with a tribal chieftain who wants to extend his holdings and sets out to plunder his neighbors. The victims of those incursions get together to protect themselves against the raider. They soon recognize that one has an abundance of something which the other can use and trade bonds are formed. Over the years, as alliances are formed and broken, villages take sides and change sides. Gradually power gravitates to centers which come to dominate large areas of the country and control shifts from the individual villages. Power itself shifts from one area to another and the language shifts with it. Dialects move from one part of the country to another, meet, blend, and change. There is no way to tell exactly when "English" emerges as a separate tongue distinct from the Germanic dialects which spawned it, just as there is no way to know why, with the Saxons dominating, the language comes to be called English after the more obscure Angles. Make no mistake about it, there is still no national language. Individual dialects command relatively small areas so that villagers from one area may understand villagers from another only with great difficulty or not at all.

2

Enter the Vikings . . .

Around the end of the eighth century, Viking raiders begin to probe the coast of England. These early raids are of little consequence (unless of course you live in one of the villages being sacked). In the middle of the ninth century, the Vikings attack in force and, after a series of battles, control of the northern part of England is ceded to them. The affect on the language is enormous. The Vikings seem to have no more proprietary interest in their language than the Germanic tribes which came before them. In some areas the inhabitants are speaking an English dialect, in others they are speaking a Scandinavian dialect and in others, a combination of both. Not only are words changinhg, but also structure. Differences between the northern and southern dialects become more pronounced.

And more Vikings . . .

While one group of Vikings flex their muscles in England, another group settle in the north of France. They abandon their roots almost entirely and adopt the local French customs and language. Known as Normans, they conquer England two hundred years later, in 1066. The language of the rulers of England is now a provincial French dialect; English is left for the peasants.

It is at this point that English gains a class distinction of sorts. Craftsmen and scholars are now coming from France bringing the language of their trades with them. French words are now used to describe the workings of the elite scholars, artists and craftsmen.

English, without official recognition, left to the Englanders, is changing dramatically. Regional differences are more pronounced with seemingly arbitrary differences in vocabulary, spelling, and grammar. Most important, the language is becoming a lot simpler. Lacking the guiding hand of scholars to point out the error of their ways, peasants are dropping the arbitrary genders and inflectional endings, in short, the unnecessary complications which have up until now plagued "correct" speech.

As the ruling Normans become increasingly isolated from the continent, they begin to think of themselves more as Englishmen than Frenchmen and English once more becomes the language of the land. Intermarriage plays a great part in the transition, for, as one scholar observes, "the children learn French from their fathers and English from their mothers." For many years, French will remain the official language, the language of the courts and parliament.

3

For even more years, informal communication will swing back and forth casually between the two languages, often in the same sentence, without affectation.

By the middle of the fifteenth century, thousands of French words have been adopted into English. In the year 1490, William Caxton prints the first book in English and recounts in the preface the story of a person traveling fifty miles who can not make himself understood when asking for food. It will be another century before that kind of situation is unusual.

By the time of Columbus' first voyage, English is the dominant language in England, but not until the time of Shakespeare and the voyage of the Pilgrims is it a language that can be understood by most Englishmen.

The English are not shy about coining new words (Shakespeare alone adds about 2000 words to the language) or borrowing from others. The practice continues as English goes abroad.

LET'S GO TO AMERICA

Words for a New World

When English travels to America, it begins to change almost as soon as it gets off the boat. Native American words, often shortened and modified, are borrowed to name unfamiliar wildlife and plants (*moose, hickory, squash, opossum, persimmon*). Settlers moving west feel that *meadow* doesn't describe the Great Plains and so *prairie* is borrowed from the French explorers. The furious snowstorms that blow down from the Rocky Mountains like a volley of shot are called by the word which means just that — *blizzard* — a usage that not only sticks, but finds its way back to England.

Words for a New Government

Politics plays a part in development of the language as well. The American legislative body is called *congress* and when an adjective is needed, *congressional* is coined, a word which makes scholars cringe because of the way in which it is formed. An Algonquin Indian word for *great man* is altered to make *mugwump*, *gerrymandering* is named for the Massachusetts governor who does it when he is in office, the Spanish word for freebooter has become *filibuster*, and although Whig and Tory come from England, the *Know-nothings* are a homegrown American product.

In the Congress of 1819-21, Felix Walker delivers a long, dull speech for his home county of Buncombe, North Carolina and a new word is coined. How ironic that *bunkum* and *bunk* are introduced by a member of Congress.

Words for a New Nation

The patriots of the American Revolution have mixed feelings about the language. Some think that a new language should be adopted to accentuate the split with England. Many who do not agree, fear that the influx of non-English speakers and the scattered pockets of settlers will not only alter the language but create a diversity of dialects which will undermine attempts to unify the nation. What is happening is that the language is being enriched by borrowing from the languages brought in by immigrants.

The Dutch settling in the Hudson River valley bring *boss, coleslaw* and *stoop*. The Germans in Pennsylvania give us *loafer, sauerkraut* and *noodle*. From the French in Louisiana comes *levee, portage* and *gopher*. The Spanish/Mexicans add *adobe, corral, hoosegow* and *vamoose*. Everyone brings something to the party and we all go home linguistically richer.

Culturally, the new nation is different from the old and shows it most in names for government offices and occupations, though there are other areas where terminology differs such as parts of an automobile and railway terms. The status of certain words or change in shades of meaning highlight cultural differences as well.

And more words for today

Changes in lifestyle, changes in awareness, changes in taste and changes in technology constantly bring new words into the language. Some of the words are new or newly borrowed, and many are just new to us.

Words like *sushi, sashimi, tofu, miso* and *nori* are reserved for aficionados of Japanese cooking until they became part of our pop culture and our language.

The word *ecology* is not new, but it doesn't become a part of everyday vocabulary until it becomes a political issue.

The computer has been around for over a generation, but then so has the word processor, work station, and photo copier none of which become a part of our vocabulary until they become an integral part of our lives. You may not know how a chip works or be able to define what it is, but you know what it is. You may not have an answering machine, camcorder or a VCR, but you know someone who does and all of those become part of our everyday vocabulary.

Popular culture coins new words or changes the meanings of old ones. Some of the words and meanings stick, some disappear almost as fast as they arrive.

There you have it — a brief summary of fifteen hundred years of linguistic evolution. We now have in America a collection of words that are generally understood throughout the land.

THE WORLD'S GREATEST VOCABULARY

Where has it gotten us?

The Oxford English Dictionary defines over 600,000 words! It has been estimated that scientific and technical terms amount to four or five times that number. Over three million words in total. Probably more when you consider that there are over a million names for insects alone. The weight of words is staggering.

Estimates vary widely as to how many words we know and how many we use. We may recognize as many as 50,000 words, although we would be hard pressed to define most of them. We often appreciate the context in which a word is used and understand without the ability to recite a precise definition. No problem, as long as we derive the meaning which is intended. Legal documents which spell out every facet of a subject in great detail and which should serve to clarify usually do quite the opposite, unless that is your area of expertise. If it isn't, and you truly want to understand what you're reading, you need a dictionary close at hand.

Of all those words we know, we probably use less than 3,000 on a regular basis. We might conclude from this that we not inclined to be adventurous in our speaking and writing; we fall into certain patterns and make little effort to change them.

Using even 3,000 words well can be formidable when you consider that the precise meaning of a word often changes over time and knowing the familiar definition may not be enough to adequately express a thought so that another person understands exactly what you mean.

And where are we going?

Anyone interested in the ways in which the language is changing need only read a newspaper or a news magazine. Even a staid old newspaper with its own style manual can not escape linguistic changes reflected in news stories, reviews or columnists' opinions.

As for those of us who use the language, hopefully we're going to make better use of the words which we know and gain the use of those with which we have only a passing acquaintance.

The way in which we use words has the same checkered past as the words themselves. The rules of grammar presented as inviolable are every bit as arbitrary as a word adopted from one source, modified by a prefix from another and a suffix from yet another. Structure is most important in forming a message that can be readily understood by another; nevertheless, there are rules devised only to suit a scholarly whim. It is well to know the difference.

Finally . . .

Enjoy! Don't let the language intimidate you. The more you learn, the more fun it becomes. You gain control, because you know that none of it was handed down on stone tablets. You realize that words were coined and massaged by people like us. (Perhaps a little smarter . . . perhaps not.)

Who knows but that you might introduce something new into the language. Changing a word a little or combining a couple of words to better suit your need strikes someone else who borrows and passes it on and then someone else borrows it and then . . . fifty years from now someone will agonize over its meaning and say "What fool . . .?"

If you want to know more . . .

For a very readable, informative and amusing tour through the history of the English language, the origin of words, etc. find a copy of *The Mother Tongue: English & How It Got That Way*, by Bill Bryson, published by William Morrow and Company.

Also recommended is an excellent book on the development of American English, *Our Own Words*, by Mary Helen Dohan, published by Penguin Books.

Part II
Escape from High School English

Escape from High School English

Writing and speaking in the classroom is extremely important, because we know that if it isn't done well it may be done again next semester. Unfortunately, that is often the only impression we retain except, perhaps, relief when it's over. Compulsory English courses are taught in a vacuum — basic grammar as though the language was created around a set of rules; great literature just because it's there with no explanation of why it is considered great.

The chances are slight that anyone will ever explain how the language was formed and, beyond disapproval of grammatically incorrect advertising slogans, how it continues to change and grow. No one mentions that you don't have to like Shakespeare to appreciate the color and power he brought to the language. Most important, little emphasis is placed on the primary function of language as a tool for communicating; work is judged on proper technique, not content.

It's time to escape. Time to view the rules of grammar as guidelines, helpful as long as they don't interfere with communication. Time to be more concerned with what we say than whether or not we say it properly. Time to express ourselves; to put our own mark on what we say and write.

THE IMPORTANCE OF COMMUNICATING WELL

> **Every time you speak or write, someone makes a judgment about you before even considering what is you have to say.**

Most of us like ourselves the way we are and feel that others should accept us as we are; however, that's not realistic, for life is comprised of a series of brief encounters. Think about it. You may spend a lot of time with family members and a few close friends, while most of the people you know are little more

9

than passing acquaintances. You make judgments about them based on brief encounters, just as they make judgments about you and who can tell what we're really like based on a brief encounter?

> You're absorbed in discussion with your colleagues. Someone you don't know approaches, listens for a bit, then attempts to join in. The way you interpret the first statement that person makes is dominated by your prejudices. An emphatic statement causes you to admire that person as decisive . . . or to resent the interruption of a know-it-all. A hesitant delivery checkered with pauses to search for words creates the image of someone who is diplomatic . . . or wishy-washy . . . or simply trying to ease into the group, though fearful of disapproval. Vocabulary and pronunciation further reinforce your first impression. The visual impression adds to the impact; whether overdressed or too casual, you see a snob, a sophisticate, an intellectual or an artist. A fool in a $600 suit is still a fool, but you perceive him differently because he is certainly no ordinary fool.

Now turn it around. You are the stranger approaching the group. How are you perceived? How do you *want* to be perceived?

You have just one chance

Fortunately, in the scenario described above there will probably be ample opportunity to correct (or confirm) the first impression. All too often, in your most important encounters, you will not be afforded that luxury. If you doubt this, consider how many times you have heard statements like these:

> "We met last week and you created a terrible impression, but I'd like to get together again to see if we have anything in common."

> "We received your letter of June 3, which was so garbled that we couldn't understand it and wonder if you would mind stopping by to explain further."

> "We couldn't make any sense out of your report on the Briscoe situation, but several members did fall asleep and wonder if you would mind delivering it again next week."

When you first meet someone you think you would like to know better, you need to leave that person with the impression that you are worth knowing. A letter applying for a job has to convince the recipient that it is worthwhile to at least talk to you. On a job interview, you have to come across as the person who should be considered for the position. A letter to sell your idea or product must describe exactly what you are selling and why the buyer should give it more than passing consideration. A report, whether written or oral, should clearly define the subject (or problem), relate the pertinent facts and outline conclusions without confusing the reader.

One chance is often all you get to make the right impression: the impression that you could be a good friend, that you could fit into the workplace, that you are ready for a promotion. It is in your best interest to be certain that you make the best possible use of that one chance.

Improving communication does not mean changing the way you are; it means learning to express yourself so that others will receive a favorable first impression and give your thoughts and ideas a fair hearing. After that, it is up to you.

ELEMENTS OF EFFECTIVE COMMUNICATION

Effective communication requires a sender with a message and the ability to convey that message in such a way that the receiver reacts in precisely the way intended by the sender.

If you want to communicate effectively, consider the main elements in the above statement: the message, you (the sender), the receiver and your intent.

The message

Of course you know what it is you want to convey, but this is the place where you dot the i's and cross the t's. Be certain that what you say is in fact the message you want to deliver.

What are we dealing with here? your place in the cosmos, your reliability as an employee or your skills? your company's entire product line or a single

11

product? the evil that men do or just one mistake, one time, on one order? an idea for world peace or just a way to get along with the guy in the next cubicle?

Be specific. Applying for a position, you need to determine whether you want to sell your experience, the perception of you as a member of a team or both. When you sell a product, decide whether to sell price, consistency, service or something else. When you sell a service, do you sell your company's reputation for service or your own? When you want to resolve a complaint, do you concentrate on the specific problem or the feeling that you aren't paying enough attention to the client? Do you press the company to solve a problem by focusing on cost, lost revenues or the importance of a particular customer? A report to your boss outlining a new procedure is not an invitation to write a history of the company (unless that's what he or she wants).

Be relevant. It may be difficult to remain focused, but it is certainly important if you want to get your message across without confusing your audience. Your perfect attendance record at lodge meetings is not going to carry as much weight as your skills when you apply for a job as an electrician and nobody but you cares that you meditate to Ravel's Bolero. On the other hand, having a clean sheet with the IRS and the local constabulary will be of importance when you apply for a job as treasurer. A report about a critical error in a shipment to a customer does not require a list of all errors made by the company since the beginning of time, but statistics about similar errors might be relevant if they relate to suggestions for avoiding a recurrence. Similarly, the customer doesn't want to hear about your superior product and your wonderful past record; however, there may be interest in how this happened and why you are sure it won't happen again.

You can broaden your message and still be relevant. If you are applying for a position which has been advertised, or responding to a request for information, you already have a good idea of what your audience wants; however, you may find it worthwhile to provide additional information. In a letter applying for a position you don't list your complete job history, but you may want to mention your experience and success in related areas. You won't be the first person hired for a job other than the one for which you applied. The response to a request for information about credit terms wouldn't be complete without mention of discounts for fast payment; information about a product should also include at least brief mention of similar products which you have available.

You, the messenger

You are the person with a message. You have appointed yourself the person to deliver the message. Can you do it? Are you sure you want to do it?

Of course you can do it, but don't be slow to to assess yourself and your abilities as an important part of the process. Remember, the goal is not the doing, it is the result, and you need to be sure that you can achieve the desired result.

Don't be shy about asking for help from someone who knows. People are always flattered to be asked, whether they show it or not. Have someone whose opinion you respect critique your letter or your notes for a speech. It can't hurt and it will probably help. Someone you know with the technical expertise which you need may bore the life out of you, but that person may also give you exactly the information you need to accomplish your purpose. And as a fringe benefit, you just might alter your perspective and make a new friend.

Don't oversell yourself, promising a lot more than you can deliver; if the truth isn't readily apparent, it will be, and probably sooner that you like. On the other hand, don't undersell yourself; make certain that the recipient knows exactly what it is that you *can* do, particularly if you have something to offer that others may not have.

Can you deliver in such a way that your audience will receive? You may be great at spouting technical jargon, but can you deliver an understandable message to an audience which lacks the technical background? Conversely, can you deliver a simple message with enough impact to register with a more knowledgeable audience. Can you deliver a sensitive message in such a way that emotion will not blur the message?

Approach the challenge with confidence. An old sales adage says that the most under-reported crime is underpricing. Now change that to read "undervaluing." Whether you are selling yourself or your product, have confidence in yor message and your ability to deliver that message. Know that when you clearly define the options, your audience cannot fail to understand that dealing with you is the only reasonable decision.

The receiver, your audience

Now that you know what you want to say and you know you can say it, you had better hope someone is listening. You may have an unknown audience or one which you know too well. How well you assess that audience determines whether or not you have wasted your time.

Consider the point of view of your audience, whether you are job hunting, selling a product, soothing a wounded ego or simply passing along information.

If you are trying to reach someone who does not know or care that you exist, you need to establish quickly that you have a product, a talent or something which is of value to that person, whereas a message to an old friend will probably open with a bit of familiar banter which confirms that you are still friends.

Are you trying to reach someone who is very busy (or should be)? Express your appreciation that he or she is taking time out of a busy schedule to respond to you.

Is this person familiar with your business? If not, you want to avoid technical terms which may be misunderstood.

Is a customer angry about a lost shipment or damaged merchandise? Don't begin by saying "It's no big deal." (Even if it is no big deal.) Present the facts, along with a solution, and let your customer decide.

Focus on the needs of your audience. People buying insurance don't care how much insurance you sold last year; they want to know how reliable you are when they have a claim. Tell busy people how you can save them time and frugal people how you can save them money.

Whether you are addressing a prospective employer, a prospective client or a group of co-workers, your message is of interest only to the extent that it can satisfy their needs. You have to make a judgment about what those needs are. If you guess wrong, you have to decide to take a different approach or recognize that you are addressing the wrong audience. A course in how to get rich in three easy lessons or one hard one is of no interest to someone who is already rich or doesn't care to be rich (or who is convinced you don't know what you're talking about).

Take advantage of feedback. When the boss mentions that he let someone go for being rude to a customer, don't tell the story about the argument you had with another customer. Sounds dumb to even mention it, but — it happens! Salesmen tell angry customers horror stories about problems or near misses. Job applicants talk about how they conned the boss at their last job. These are clearly people who are not listening and certainly not thinking.

Advertising agencies spend millions building profiles of prospective buyers for a product, then convince their clients to spend hundreds of millions more wooing that prospect; yet they often target the wrong market. You don't have millions, so do the best you can and you will probably be right as often as the professionals.

Your intent; the response you want

It's a bit glib to say you want a favorable response. Of course you do! But what is a favorable response? A pat on the head and a hearty "Well done"?

Here's where you put it all together. Is your intent to instruct? to inform? to persuade? to intimidate?

Whatever your goal, keep it in mind when you evaluate your message, the way you deliver that message and your audience.

If you are trying to convince a friend to take a college course to prepare for a promotion, decide whether your concern is about the course or the promotion. Can you think of other benefits of taking the course, whether or not the promotion becomes a reality? Are there ways to get the promotion without taking the course? Either way, set your sights and don't get side tracked.

Before telling someone how to do a job, focus on what you want to accomplish. Do you want that person to be able to immediately handle the task alone, or to simply grasp the concept of what needs to be done with you standing by ready to assist when necessary?

Do you need to convince your boss that you want a meeting to discuss a project? Then don't get so wrapped up in describing what you want to discuss at the meeting that minds are made up before the meeting takes place.

Are you sending out a memo which requires adherence to a procedure "or else"? If your intent is to be laughed at, this will do it. If compliance is your goal, be sure you have a specific punishment which fits the crime of non-compliance. (Incidentally, when you are being intimidating, it's not a bad idea to take a second look to be sure you are also being fair and rational; fifty lashes for wasting paper clips is not fair or rational.

Focus clearly on your purpose and stick with it, but do be sensible. Don't emulate the fellow who wouldn't take "yes" for an answer until the proper place in his presentation by which time his listener was so annoyed that he got a "no".

Be ready to shift gears when the response to your message doesn't meet your expectations. You can tell how well you are doing by the reaction to your message. When you don't get the anticipated response, be ready to do some fancy footwork. If your proposal is met with, "It can't be done," don't try to bully your way through the discussion. It's time to let the other person talk and if you listen well, there is an excellent chance you'll be given the answers you need to modify your presentation.

TOOLS FOR EFFECTIVE COMMUNICATION

Elsewhere in this book is a section called **Basic Grammar**, a compendium of the rules and notions which classify words as parts of speech as well as dictating sentence structure, punctuation, capitalization and such. An understanding of grammar is certainly an aid to communicating well, not so much for the rules themselves, but for the insight it can give into structuring our communication to be universally understood. This section might be described as an ante-grammar — a preface to the more formal structure of our communication.

Words, and the shades of meaning

Most of us use less than three thousand different words on a regular basis. However many words you use, they may not be adequate to properly express your thoughts all of the time. So how do you learn new words? You might try the old system of selecting a word from the dictionary and using it until you remember it. If it doesn't work, at least friends who recognize what you are doing will find it amusing.

To improve the way in which you express thoughts and ideas, look first at the words you use. Develop an awarenes of words used repeatedly and find replacements for them. Whenever appropriate, use replacements which are more colorful or descriptive. In all probability, the overused word does not always convey your message precisely, it just gets used out of habit; therefore, look for a word which will convey to your listener a more exact image, if possible.

Where are the new words? Well, it seems that we recognize more than ten times the number of words we use. Good place to start. Try to think of familiar words which are not normally a part of your vocabulary. Look them up, if you have to, to be sure of their meaning. Mental block? A good Thesaurus will give you synonyms for the word you are trying to replace and with any luck, at least a few will be familiar words that you don't ordinarily think to use. A peripheral benefit is that once you've jump started a few brain cells this way, more of them kick in and you begin to remember words you didn't think you knew. Spooky, huh?

Be selective about the words you use. Every grammarian has a pet peeve about words that are trite, in bad taste or used improperly. What you use is strictly up to you, but you should consider your audience. Years ago, Louis Armstrong described a concert he gave in England when George V was king. Despite a warning that it was a breach of etiquette to acknowledge the monarch's presence, Louis said that before playing one of the king's favorites, he looked up at the royal box, "And I said, 'This one's for you, Rex.' and I laid *You Rascal You* on him." He could do that; you can't, unless you play a great horn.

Colloquialisms can be effective, but not if they diminish your status in your listener's mind. Conversely, obscure words which do not fit you or your style can leave the impression that you are talking down to your audience.

Be alert to changes in the use of words. *Lady* and *gentleman* once indicated social status; today they are mostly used ironically or pejoratively. *Lady* in particular has fared badly in the last generation, from *my old lady* referring to a wife, then to a female companion, to banishment by those who want to shed the image of the frail dependent creature which the word *lady* suggests. You may not be beheaded for calling a king "Rex," but misuse of *lady* could point you in that direction. *Babe* or *girl* as an address for a woman past her majority might also satisfy any curiosity you have about drawing and quartering.

Avoid superfluous words. Fight the temptation to use two words meaning the same thing or almost the same thing when one will do the job or to indicate a comparison of something which represents an absolute such as *unique, perfect* or *full*.

In *actual fact*, **the job was done well.** *Actual* means existing in fact; a *fact* is anything actually existent.

again and again, over and over — Repetition can emphasize, but don't use it unless it does help.

all and sundry — *All* pretty much covers it.

They were *all united* in song. *United* makes the point unless, of course, they were singing *Happy Birthday* which is never sung in unison (or the same key).

He accepted *any and all* challenges. *All* covers it nicely; don't say more unless you really feel you need to make a point.

best of the best — May be acceptable for advertising copy hyping a professional wrestling match, but nothing else.

This is the *most deadly* (or *most lethal*) poison available. Watch out for this one, it can be deadly. *Deadly* and *lethal* both mean "liable or certain to cause death," and it's difficult to imagine being more dead as opposed to less dead except in colloquial expressions; however, there is a tendency to characterize a poison or illness as more liable to cause death or to cause death quicker. Hardly worth a great deal of discussion, except that there are other words which may cause similar difficulty. (See the next example.)

This is the *most square* board I have. The board is either square or not square. Presumably we are selecting from a number of boards which are not square and have chosen the board which is *most nearly square.* Same goes for **round**.

down in the ground, up in the sky — Trust me, we won't dig up in the ground if you promise not to fly down in the sky.

We *estimate* that *about* (or *approximately*) half the people voted. An estimate *is* an approximation.

She received a *great big* package. As opposed to a great small package, like a diamond, maybe?

huge giant — Perhaps a huge giant of a man needs to be differentiated from a small giant of a man, but it's doubtful.

They were *joined together* in marriage. Joined is enough; perhaps in a few years they will be joined apart.

little tiny — Like the giants, little tiny things probably need to be kept separate from big tiny things.

most unique — *Unique* is without equal, singular, one of a kind and cannot be compared to another.

one and the same — Can something be one and different?

She gave the *oral* report *verbally* to the entire committee. Beats having to write it all down orally; this one got printed, honest.

over and above — Perhaps over and under are one and different.

That's the *most perfect* dress I've seen. There may be many perfect things floating around out there, but they can't be compared; one is not more perfect than another.

planned in advance — Planning is a thing you do in advance; it's either planned or nothing was done in advance.

This is far from a complete list of potential sins; you have to go out and commit some of your own. The old saw says "Think before you speak." Better add, "Think about the words before you use them."

Use words that enhance your message, not detract from it.

Organizing words into coherent thoughts

A sentence is described as a group of words that expresses a complete thought. Much better to think of it as expressing a "coherent thought."

For information about the mechanics of sentence structure such as the parts which make up a sentence and types of sentences, see **Basic Grammar, Sentence Structure.** In this section we are primarily interested in the manner in which sentence structure colors your communication.

The English language affords us considerable flexibility to express our thoughts. We can make a series of concise statements which, taken together, form a complete picture . . .

> **They saw a truck. The truck was blue. It raced through the center of town. The truck was followed by a police car. The police car had its siren on.**

. . . we can wrap it all up together in a single package . . .

> **They saw the blue truck race through the center of town followed by a police car with its siren on.**

and we can make it confusing.

> **Racing through the center of town, they saw the police car following the blue truck with its siren on.**

Who's racing? and who has the siren? and we really don't talk or write like that, do we? DO WE? . . . Sometimes.

Sentence structure and repetition can set the tone of a communication:

> **Make sure the job gets done and while you're at it, get me a status report.**

> **Make sure the job gets done. Make sure it gets done now. And get me a status report.**

The first sentence above gets the message across with less sense of urgency and demand than the shorter sentences. The short statements are designed to punctuate the consciousness of the listener.

A longer sentence with a smooth flow which doesn't jolt the reader or listener presents the voice of reason, a logical presentation of information, as long as it doesn't become convoluted and confusing.

The longer sentence which recounts a series of events, elicits yet another image:

> **She ran down the hill, jumped the fence, and dashed across the field.**

> **The containers are sterilized, filled with liquid, capped, labeled and packed in boxes.**

An orderly, if somewhat breathless, account. A different approach might be two or more sentences with more descriptive information.

Use the style that gets the emotional response you want and make sure that the message is clear.

Punctuation, capitalization, and other demons

The only important rules of punctuation and capitalization are the ones which clarify your message.

A period, question mark or exclamation point at the end of a sentence tells the reader that your thought is completed. (Hopefully, to start up again before you begin the next sentence.)

The comma is an aid to understanding when used to separates items which might otherwise run together and create confusion. When you are in doubt about where to put a comma, say the sentence aloud. Place a comma where a pause is natural, where it is needed to separate a thought or a list of items. Be careful though that you don't get carried away and interfere with the flow of the thought. Use your best judgment, and you will usually be right.

Aside from the customary capitalization such as at the beginning of a sentence and a proper name, avoid the gratuitous use of capital letters except for a good reason. If the monthly meeting of the board of directors of your company is referred to in hushed tones, you may want to capitalize any reference to the Board Meeting in your correspondence. After all, these are not people you want to offend.

When in doubt as to whether a product is generic or proprietary, capitalize to be on the safe side; companies are protective of their trade names and erring on the side of caution is not likely to be criticized. Kleenex passed into our generic lexicon long ago, but any reference to the tissue had better be capitalized if you expect Kimberly-Clark to look favorably on any correspondence.

For more information about punctuation, capitalization and stuff like that, see **Basic Grammar.** In the meantime, use your own good judgment.

You don't need to know the parts of speech — but it helps

This is the toughest one to sell — it won't make you the life of the party, it won't even help you get invited to the party and it won't grow hair, but it is worthwhile to know something about the parts of speech.

21

Your ability to write and speak well doesn't depend on a thorough knowledge of the rules of grammar, but it helps to understand how words are used properly in order to avoid using them improperly. Make sure you know at least as much as your recipient about proper use of the language to avoid having him or her make any unfounded, nasty judgments about you based on the style of your presentation rather than its content.

ABOUT COMPUTERS AND WORD PROCESSORS

Just in case you've been asleep in a cave for the past ten years, it's time you knew — there aren't many typewriters around anymore. The word processor is replacing the typewriter and lest you think it's just more beaurocratic jargon like "maintenance engineer" for janitor, let's clarify the terms.

Overview of equipment and programs

The **word processor** is a computer dedicated to word processing functions such as translating key strokes to an internal memory, allowing editing of typed copy and printing the information stored. The word processor works much like a typewriter, except that entries from the keyboard appear on a small screen and are not transferred to paper until the operator activates a command to print. This allows the operator to review and edit the material before printing.

Word processors are generally unitized, that is, the keyboard, computer, screen and printer are all contained in a single piece of equipment about the size of a typewriter.

Capabilities of the machines vary widely. Some allow working with only one line at a time; others save a full page or more for subsequent editing. Some can only retain a document in memory while it is being processed; others accommodate an external storage device such as a floppy disk on which work can be saved for future editing. Some print in a single typewriter-style font, including bold and italics; others offer several fonts comprising different faces and sizes. All are programmed internally, that is, whatever the capabilities for editing and printing, they are part of the machine and cannot be changed. Some offer the operator assistance with vocabulary and spelling (see **Special help . . .**, below).

Generally, word processors are less expensive and take less space than a computer, but they have a more limited capability.

The **computer** referred to in this context is the micro-mini computer, desktop computer or personal computer, whichever term you prefer. They all apply to the same class of machine.

The personal computer is made up of several connecting elements comprising the CPU or central processing unit (which usually includes internal and external data storage capabilities), the keyboard, the monitor or screen and the printer.

The computer has the capability to perform a variety of tasks for which there are thousands of applications available. Because of this versatility, applications are not normally programmed into the system but are purchased separately according to the preference of the user.

Word processing applications for the computer cover a wide range in terms of cost and sophistication from simple typewriter emulation to desktop publishing with print quality type and graphics.

Correcting and editing

One of the main attractions of the word processor or the computer is the ability to edit work before printing thereby eliminating troublesome erasures. Those which have the capacity to save work for editing at a later date are most desirable because they allow corrections and updates for subsequent printing.

All but the simplest systems allow the copying of data from one document to another so that a standard paragraph can be typed once and used in other documents without retyping.

Many applications also have the capability to merge a file of names and addresses with a single document so that multiple copies of the document will be personalized for each recipient.

Special help with spelling, grammar and vocabulary

Most systems, particularly those which are computer-based, will check the document for correct spelling.

Some of the more sophisticated systems check for grammatical and other errors such as typing *as* for *is* or the improper use of words like *to, too* and *two*.

Some applications will hyphenate at the end of lines to avoid a ragged look.

Vocabulary options allow the user to call up synonyms and antonyms as possible substitutes for a word.

Caution! — don't get lazy. It's easy to take advantage of your application's capability and disregard the fact that it does not reflect your style. Be sure to check the computer's work carefully; you may not agree with the grammar or hyphenation system. Some of the programs are user sensitive and attempt to emulate your style by remembering when you override hyphenation or grammar suggestions; remember, however, that your style may change, and if you don't check up on the computer's work, it will never know.

Organizing and saving your files

When you first begin to save files, whether on a fixed disc in the computer or on external media such as floppies, you can't imagine ever having difficulty locating a document. Wrong. Bad thought! Bad thought! Wipe it out of your memory banks now!

Directories. The computer allows you to create directories (think of them as file folders) in which you can store your work. Some programs start you off with one data directory in which your work is stored to keep it separate from the program files. Based on the kind of work you are doing, decide how you want to organize your files. You may want to set up a directory for each client, for financial reports, sales reports, production reports, love letters, etc.

Files. These are the documents which you create. Some systems limit you to a combination of eight letters and numbers for the document name, some allow more. Decide how you want to organize the files within a directory so that you can easily retrieve them from a list in alpha-numeric order. You may want to include in the name a code for easy identification by type of document (letter, price bid, report) and when it was created. Establishing an orderly system which makes access and identification easy will be of immense help when you back up your work and when you need to reorganize. A system will allow you to manipulate groups of files instead of individual documents.

We make jokes about things "lost in the computer" until, like Walt Kelly's Pogo, "We has met the enemy and they is us."

There are books and applications with loads of information to keep you from tearing out your hair when you need help, so we won't go into any further detail beyond this brief warning — organize as though you are setting up a system to handle all of the data for a major corporation! The time you spend organizing at the beginning is nothing compared to the time and headache of trying to reorganize if your system proves inadequate in six months.

WORD PROCESSING TERMS

access To call up for revision or printing.

application Any task performed by the word processor or computer.

backup or **backup copy** An extra copy of programs or data made for protection against the loss of the original as a result of power failure, machine malfunction, etc.

batch printing The ability to line up multiple documents to print in sequence automatically, usually simultaneous with the creation or editing of other documents.

boilerplate Standardized copy which can be called up for insertion in documents as needed.

bold or **bold face** Type which is darker than the normal font; depending on the system, bold face may be a special font or it may be created by overtyping in the same font.

center The command which automatically centers a line of type between the margins or on a tab stop.

character Anything typed to print out plus the control characters which carry formatting instructions for the document. Normally, only the material which prints is visible on the screen, although most systems offer a view mode which allows viewing of the control characters.

copy May refer to the contents of a document; a duplicate of the document; the act of reproducing data under another name or to another disk (see **back up**); the act of reproducing a portion of a document elsewhere in the document or in another document (see also, **boilerplate, cut**)

control character See **character**.

continuous forms Forms which are attached in a continuous stream for feeding through a word processor or printer, perforated for separation after printing. Continuous forms may be plain bond, letterheads, invoices, checks, envelopes, etc.

CPU (central processing unit) The main part of the computer or word processing system which contains main memory and instructions to carry out system control functions.

create To start a new document with a distinctive name for identification.

CRT (Cathode Ray Tube) The viewing screen; also called *visual*

display or *video display*.

cursor The on-screen indicator which shows where the next typed character will be entered.

cursor keys Special keys which move the cursor to a new position without changing anything else on the screen.

cut or **cut and paste** The ability to delete copy from a document and move it to another place in the document or to another document.

decimal alignment The ability to line up numbers in a column on a decimal point, usually a function of a tab setting.

default or **default settings** The settings, such as margins, which are built into the system as the standard format settings unless other settings are specified.

directory A division of the disk filing system which holds a group of files.

disk A device for storing data. A *fixed* or *hard* disk is usually housed within the computer or word processor. A *floppy* disk, also called a *diskette* is an external device which is inserted into a slot in the machine called a **disk drive.**

dot matrix printer A printer which uses dots to make up the image of letters and graphics. Quality of output varies from standard computer print to letter quality.

draft printer A dot-matrix printer which produces low-quality output suitable only for internal reports and files. (See also, **letter quality** and **near-letter quality**.)

edit keys Function keys or key combinations which perform editing functions such as *cut and paste*; *delete* character, word or line; *go to* next word, line or page; *format* type, etc.

enter key May be used to signify the end of a line similar to the carriage return on a typewriter. In those systems where the word processor or computer determines the line ending, the enter key is pressed at the end of a paragraph or to force a line break. Also used as a signal to execute some commands.

error message A brief on-screen message indicating that an operation cannot be performed as entered. Often accompanied by instructions for correcting.

field A part of a document or file record which is distinctly identified, usually by a name; for example, in a customer list, *last name* may be a field name and the *last name of the customer* in that record is the field.

file name The distinctive name or code assigned to a file to identify it for future use.

flush left The command which aligns text on the left hand side of the page.

flush right The command which aligns text on the right hand side of the page.

form feed The setting which tells the word processor and printer that continuous forms are being processed; that printing may proceed without delay between documents.

format Page layout specifications such as margins, tab settings, indents, line spacing, etc.

hard copy A printout on paper.

hardware The physical equipment such as the CPU, keyboard and printer.

header Text programmed to appear at the top of each page such as a title, page number or date.

highlight A feature which sets selected text apart by some means such as underlining or reversing, usually prior to formatting in some way.

hyphenation Use of the hyphen to divide a word between syllables at the end of a line of copy in order to make lines less ragged or connect the parts of a compound word.

justify The command which aligns text both left and right.

letter quality Refers to the quality of print produced by a good typewriter; the standard for judging the quality of print in business letters. (See also, **draft**

quality, near letter quality.)

line spacing The spacing between lines of printed copy, normally six lines to the inch. Some systems allow considerable control over the line spacing in a document.

merge The ability to combine elements from different files such as names and addresses from a data base file with a letter from a document file.

module One of the pieces of the hardware which make up a system, such as the printer, keyboard, etc.

monitor The screen on which work is viewed. See also, **CRT.**

NLQ, near-letter quality Dot matrix emulation of typewriter or letter quality print. (See also, **draft quality, letter quality.**)

paste A command to insert data which has been copied to a temporary file such as a clipboard. See also, **cut and paste.**

program Software. The set of instructions which enables the system to perform tasks such as word processing.

prompt A screen message which requires a response.

proportional spacing Typesetting in which the space provided for each letter is proportional to the size of the letter as compared to typewriter type which provides the same amount of space for each letter which results in distracting variations in the amount of white space between letters.

return See **enter**

scroll Moving the cursor up or down on the screen to move through the text of a document.

shared printer A system which allows more than one work station or terminal to share a printer.

software The programs and applications which enable the hardware to perform specific tasks .(See also, **hardware.**)

sort Data organized according to predetermined parameters. Document files, for example, might be sorted by name, by last save date, by size, etc.

word wrap A word processing program feature wherein text too long for a single line wraps to the next line.

work station Minimally, the keyboard and monitor connected to a remote printer and CPU or mainframe. Often has some computer capability and a disk drive.

Part III
Basic Grammar - Putting It All Together

Basic Grammar — Putting It All Together

Those of us convinced that English 101 was created only
as an instrument of torture don't have to
worry about it anymore. Right?

Thus far we've been dealing in the abstract — the transformation of English from tribal dialect to the language we speak today, the techniques of effective communication and finally, the use of some modern tools including word processors and computers.

Presumably, your purpose in reading this book is to communicate more effectively; therefore, we cannot escape a discussion of the of the basic elements which make up the language — the way in which random words are put together to form coherent thoughts. Surely you know something about grammar (probably more than you realize) or you wouldn't be able to communicate at all. Learning more, or putting a name to that which you know, will better equip you to critically assess your writing and speaking.

It may seem that categorizing words and analyzing sentences is strictly the work of scholars for some unknown purpose. In fact, it's a tool we can all use, not just to improve our communication but to make it more powerful; *it affects the way in which we view the things we say.* As we study the words that form our sentences and the sentences that form our thoughts and ideas, we begin to understand why something expressed in a certain way is crystal clear, while the same thing expressed in another way is vague, indistinct or even misleading. How it happens is not easily explained; it's magic. Like riding a bicycle. One minute you're faltering, concentrating on staying up to avoid making a fool of yourself in front of the entire neighborhood and the next minute you're riding, wondering what all the fuss was about.

Phrases
Phrases are discussed more completely in the section describing **Sentence Structure**. In this section, a phrase refers simply to the part of a sentence being discussed or a part of speech and the words associated with it.

PARTS OF SPEECH

In order to describe how words are used in the communication of ideas, all of the words in the language have been grouped into categories called parts of speech. Each category has its own set of guidelines for use of the words in the group. The eight parts of speech are as follows:

noun	pronoun	verb	adjective
adverb	preposition	conjunction	interjection

Not all words fit neatly into a single category; many are used in more than one way and are identified with the part of speech representing the particular way in which they are being used. Our interest is always in the way the word is being used in order to determine whether it is being used properly.

> **This is the sort of English up with which I will not put.**
> **Winston Churchill**

Proper grammar is elusive, not because it is so very difficult, but because the rules are frequently arbitrary and outdated. Perhaps it is, as someone said, "because the language is so alive and those who attempt to regulate its use are so dead." There is no doubt that guidelines make it easier to study and learn the language. It is, however, unfortunate that some guidelines have become rules which make no contribution to improving communication but often do an excellent job of confusing the communicator. The admonition not to end a sentence with a preposition, for example, was first put forth by a grammarian expressing his own preference. Eventually it became a rule which even Mr. Churchill laughed at. (Oops.) Among the frequently violated rules are some which seem reasonable, such as the use of *bigger* or *heavier* to compare two things and *biggest* or *heaviest* to compare more than two, but there is no way to misunderstand when the wrong word is used, so why the rule?

There seems to be general agreement about the parts of speech and their function, but disagreement about almost everything else. Little attempt will be made here to confront those disagreements except as passing considerations.

Nouns

A noun is usually described as "a person, place or thing". That's a bit misleading because we're inclined to think of *a thing* as an inanimate object. A bird isn't a person, nor a place, nor an inanimate object (unless it's dead).

A noun is a name. It is the name we give to what we're talking about.

Person is a noun and so are all the things we call a person (you know what I mean).

> **man woman child plumber doctor manager teacher runner**
>
> **author clown lawyer baker butcher master servant chief**

Creatures, animals and **plants** are nouns as are names of all living things.

> **dog bird bug tree vegetable bloodhound wren ant fox hen**
>
> **oak spider crab gorilla pansy carrot rose godzilla cabbage**

Place and all of the places we can name,

> **home office school field street club restaurant arena**

as well as **objects**.

> **furniture tools air gold trash water teapot smoke**

There are immaterial things such as **activities,**

> **running concert cooking speech reading sewing**

and **concepts.**

> **honesty bravery theory day minute beauty**

Function of the noun

The noun may function as a subject, as an object, as an adjective or as an adverb.

The *manager* is sending *you* the *financial report* by *messenger today*.

Subject — *manager*. The subject is the lead character in this little drama. Everything in this sentence concerns the manager: he or she is sending something, sending a report, sending to you, sending it by messenger, and sending it today. Agreed?

Direct object — *report*. The direct object clarifies what is being done by naming the recipient of the action. You are the recipient of the report, but the report is recipient of the action. Clear?

Indirect object — *you*. The indirect object describes to or for whom the action is taken. It always comes before the direct object in a sentence and takes the implied preposition *to* or *for*. Okay, so it sounds confusing; think of the sentence as saying, "The manager is sending (to) you. . ." or ". . .(for) you. . ."

If the sentence is changed to read, "The manager is sending the financial report to you. . .", the word *you* would become the object of the preposition *to*. If that's not confusing enough, read on.

Object of a preposition — *messenger*. A preposition is placed before a noun or pronoun to show its relationship with another word in the sentence. In this case the preposition is *by*, the prepositional phrase is *by messenger* and it tells how the report is being sent.

Hopefully you are not going to spend a lot of time differentiating between *indirect object* and *object of a preposition*. These two may never give you a problem, but knowing the difference can help if you are unsure of something you've written.

Enough of this, but (if you are interested) there's more in the section about **Prepositions**.

Adjective –*financial*. The noun *financial* is used as an adjective to modify (or clarify) *report* so that you know what type of report is being sent. For more, see the section about **Adjectives**.

Adverb — *today*. Here we have a noun used as an adverb, answering the question *when?* which modifies the verb *sending*. More about **Adverbs** in that section as well.

Basic Grammar — Putting It All Together

Common nouns

A common noun is one which we commonly use (wonder where the name came from?) to name a non-specific thing: *dog, cat, man, woman, piano*. The examples at the beginning of this section are all common nouns because each one is a name which does not designate a specific thing.

Modifiers do not change the classification of a common noun. The noun *cat* in the phrase *my cat, Callie* remains common (though she doesn't think so), even though the reference has been narrowed down to the cat which is mine. *Callie*, however, is the name of that particular cat and a proper noun.

Proper nouns

A proper noun is a specific name and begins with a capital letter. Don't capitalize a common noun used with a proper noun unless it is part of the name. Motors which you buy from a company named General, may be described as General motors, but if you address the automobile company, it's another matter. Products from the automobile company are General Motors cars (or whatever you choose to call them based on your experience).

Identification of a proper noun is not always clear. Many names used freely as generic (or common nouns) are brand names, such as Kleenex for tissues and Vaseline for salve. Use of brand names without capitalizing is a very sensitive issue among those who hold rights to the name. Some names have become so much a part of the language that no attempt is made to preserve the proprietary right to the name. If you know the difference, capitalize; if you are not sure, look it up.

The need for capitals is not always clear. Congratulating a friend on the invention of trashfood milk supplement is going to go much further if you don't insult him by implying that it isn't worthy of capitalization.

There is also the tendency to use substitute phrases as replacements for proper names such as *The Man Upstairs* for *God* or *Big Guy* for *boss*. In the first instance, the rules for capitalizing are clear in that any reference to a particular deity is capitalized. In the second, if the company tolerates this type of reference in informal correspondence, it is well to consider that *big guy* might be viewed as an unflattering reference to the boss's physique. When in doubt, capitalize.

Collective nouns

A collective noun is a noun which refers to a collection or group as a unit and does not have a word form to describe a single member.

collection group family company orchestra herd flock

board of directors or **board**

management (not to be confused with managers)

The collective noun is singular when referring to its members as a cohesive unit and plural when referring to their diversity. In each case it is important to maintain agreement between the noun, its pronouns, if any, and its verb.

The *board* is in agreement regarding the selection of a chairman. Singular, collective — the board as a unit is in agreement.

The *members of the board* are in agreement regarding the selection of a chairman. Plural, non-collective — changing *board* to *members of the board* alters reference to the board as a unit to that of several individuals.

The *board* have different opinions regarding the selection of a chairman. Plural, collective — the *different opinions* indicate that the board as a unit is not in agreement and we have the plurality of a disunited board.

The *board members* have different opinions on the selection of a chairman. Plural, non-collective again — changing *board* to *board members* we are again considering several individuals.

Note that diversity does not indicate animosity, but only difference; you can just as easily substitute *salad dressing* for *chairman* in the examples above.

Citing all of these examples may seem redundant, but it beats reciting a bunch of rules and leaving you to figure them out. By now you have probably also noticed the best way out of difficulty — change the wording of the sentence. That is the best solution when the correct form sounds awkward to you.

Also see **Plural nouns**, below, and the section describing **Relationships**.

Plural nouns

The plural of the noun shows that you are referring to more than one.

Most noun plurals are formed by adding *s* or *es* to the singular. There are, however, many exceptions including those which change spelling,

child, children	woman, women	man, men
goose, geese	mouse, mice	die, dice
foot, feet	ox, oxen	tooth, teeth
alumnus, alumni	medium, media	datum, data
addendum, addenda	crisis, crises	

those which do not change at all,

deer hose moose sheep species vermin

and those which give you a choice.

brother	**brothers** or **brethren**
appendix	**appendixes** or **appendices**
beau	**beaus** or **beaux**
index	**indexes** or **indices**
focus	**focuses** or **foci**

The collective noun in its singular form as described above is singular when referring to the group as a single cohesive unit, plural when describing diversity. In addition, the noun itself may have a plural form.

a single **collection** of stamps or several stamp **collections**

a single **group** of people or several **groups** of people

a single **family** or several **families**

the **board of directors** of one company or the **boards of directors** of several companies, although, unless there is a need to be very specific, you are more likely to refer to **the boards** or **the directors** collectively.

The plural form of the collective noun is used in exactly the same fashion as any other plural.

> **The *boards* are in agreement regarding the selection of their chairman.** Plural, because we are talking about several *boards*, which is the same as talking about several *things*. It does not matter whether they agree, disagree or play squat tag, each board is a *thing* and the subject is more than one of those *things* which is plural and ever more shall be so. (Whew!)

Possessive nouns

The possessive noun denotes possession or ownership. It also indicates relationship, though there is some disagreement about the use of a possessive noun when referring to an inanimate object. There are those who decry the use of phrases such as **the car's top** preferring, instead, **the top which is on the car** or **the top of the car.** It's entirely up to you, for the meaning is certainly clear and no reader of suspense stories is a stranger to **the wind's howling** or **the night's impenetrable darkness.**

To show possession, add apostrophe *s* to nouns which are singular and to plurals which do not end in *s*; add only the apostrophe to plurals which end in *s*.

The great challenge when using a possessive noun is to avoid confusing plural and possessive.

> **The *boy's* bicycle is black.** Singular possessive — tells us that one boy possesses a black bicycle.

> **The *boys* bicycle every day.** Plural only — tells us that bicycling is something done by more than one boy.

> **The *boys'* bicycles are all black.** Plural possessive — tells us that more than one boy each possess a black bicycle.

> **The *boys'* bicycle is black.** Still plural possessive — tells us that there is only one bicycle, but it is in the possession of more than one boy.

To test for possessive, restructure the phrase inserting the words *of* or *belonging to.*

> **The bicycle(s) *belonging to* the boy(s).** As you can see, it works for all of the above sentences except the second.

The possessive form of collective nouns carries the same admonition to be careful not to confuse plurality with possession and, beyond that, requires only that you think about what you are trying to say.

The *group* display is effective. Singular only — *group* is a noun used as an adjective to describe the type of display.

The *group's* display is effective. Singular possessive — we are referring to the display belonging to one group.

The *group's* displays are effective. Singular possessive — this time we are referring to a single group which possesses more than one display.

The *groups'* displays are effective. Plural possessive — here we have more than one display each belonging to a different group.

Don't be discouraged; it's not as complicated as it seems. Correct usage merely requires a bit of thought and let's face it, that's one of the keys to effective communication — thinking about what you're saying.

Gender of nouns

Gender is the classification of words as **masculine**, **feminine** or none of the above, which is **neuter**. Neuter in the grammatical sense applies to words which do not make a distinction between masculine or feminine,

animal horse family parent bird bee

and those which have no sex.

rock building road car (even if you refer to it as *she*)

In English, gender is quite simple; probably no other language is as direct and rational. Old English arbitrarily assigned gender to nouns, which had to be used with the proper gender of article and adjective. If you have any doubts about how much our language is simplified by the loss of those gender nouns, browse through an English-Spanish, English-French, or English-German dictionary. The designation of a word as masculine, feminine or neuter frequently has no relation to the meaning of the word itself.

English words indicate gender in one of three ways: naming something by using one of a word pair which is different for male and female, prefacing a noun of indeterminate gender with one of those word pairs or by adding a gender-specific ending.

Some of the more familiar **word pairs** are:

male, female	man, woman	he, she
lad, lass	brother, sister	him, her
son, daughter	father, mother	uncle, aunt
nephew, niece	sir, madam	husband, wife
bull, cow	ram, ewe	stallion, mare
buck or stag, doe	rooster, hen	drake, duck
gander, goose	waiter, waitress	groom, bride
actor, actress	lord, lady	king, queen

The **gender-specific preface** is not nearly as common as in the past when it was usually a hyphenated word such as *she-lion* or *he-goat*. There are survivors, however, as in *girlfriend* and *boyfriend*, Today we are inclined to use an adjective to indicate gender such as *male secretary* or *female astronaut,* usually to describe an activity normally associated with the opposite sex. This usage is also on the decline as sex stereotypes disappear along with our wonderment that men and women do most things equally well.

Do not to confuse the gender-specific preface words with terms such as *man-hour* or *man-made* which use *man* to refer to the family of man, that is, people in general, rather than strictly male.

Gender-specific endings are few and the tendency is to avoid their use.

lion, lioness	host, hostess	count, countess
god, goddess	baron, baroness	prince, princess
usher, usherette	fiancé, fiancée	executor, executrix
aviator, aviatrix	alumnus, alumna	bachelor, bachelorette
hero, heroine	comedian, comedienne	

Okay, so what's the big deal? Why devote so much space to something described as "quite simple"?

Because I lied . . . a little. Because if you want to speak or write well you need only follow the rules, but if you want to communicate well you need to be aware of the time in which you live.

Our language has been shaped by a society which drew sharp distinctions between the strong male as hunter/provider and the weak female who stayed home to do simple things like cooking and having babies. As the role of men and women change, many take exception to the gender references and feel that they should also change. (Of course some are offended by the suggestion of change, some think it is downright silly and some don't think at all!)

The language is changing and will continue to change to reflect our society. *Chairman* is giving way to *chairperson* and *salesman* to *salesperson*. Some who feel *chairperson* is awkward, use simply *chair*; *salesperson* has evolved in some instances to *sales representative* though it can hardly be considered less awkward. There is resistance to the use of feminine endings, the feeling that *authoress* and *poetess* are condescending. Whatever your belief, you have a right to it, but be aware that insensitivity will detract from your message. More about this in the sections on **Pronouns**, **Adjectives** and **Style**.

Gender **is a term used only in grammar — usually.** *Gender* is properly used in reference to the sexual orientation of words, especially nouns and pronouns. Describing a woman as one of *the female gender* is acknowledged in some dictionaries as a humorous reference or colloquialism or both. The fact that older dictionaries don't mention this usage at all would seem to indicate a change is taking place. Be guided accordingly.

Gerund

A gerund is a verb form ending in *-ing* that can be used as a noun. This won't come up often in conversation, but you might want to know the difference.

You should *run* for exercise. *Run* is a verb, the action.

He is *running* for exercise. *Running* is still a verb, a form of *run*.

***Running* is good exercise.** Aha! the **gerund**. *Running*, a verb form of *run*, is now the noun/name of what you are talking about.

39

Pronouns

A pronoun takes the place of a noun or nouns and, therefore, represents the name we give to what we're talking about. See **Noun**, above.

Function of the pronoun

The pronoun **substitutes** for a **specific noun**, an **implied noun** or an **unknown noun**. Don't throw up your hands yet. Examples are on the way.

The **specific noun**, called the **antecedent**, is one which has been voiced (or written) previously and can now be more easily expressed as a pronoun.

> The father told *the father's daughter* that *the daughter* played better tennis than *the father* did.
>
> Kind of clumsy? You bet! Now try substituting *his, she* and *he* in the sentence.
>
> The father told *his* daughter that *she* played better tennis than *he* did.

The **implied noun** is one which has not been voiced but which is understood.

> *I* am speaking (or **writing**) and hope *you* are listening (or **reading**). *I* refers to the speaker and *you* know who you are. Whichever end of the action you are on, presence is implied, the pronouns substituting for proper names.

> If the nouns are stated rather than implied, in this kind of sentence, it comes out —I, John take you, Mary... and vice-versa

> *It* is really coming down. *It* implies something unsaid which in this case is most likely rain or snow and you should know which if you are standing in it. Would be a lot bigger news if it was going up.

The **unknown noun** is usually, but not necessarily the subject of a question.

> *Who* **is coming down the path?**
>
> *Which* **airline lost our baggage this time?**
>
> *What* **day is this?**

You certainly can't specify the subject if you don't know its name. Before you are tempted to add *when, why* or *how* to this list, see the section on **adverbs**.

Personal pronouns

These guys are important because we use them so much and we often use them incorrectly. A personal pronoun can be very impersonal, but it always refers to a person except for the pronoun *it* which may refer to something else. **The personal pronoun shows to whom or what is referring by its form.** (Stay with me on this; there will be a quiz later.)

Remember (if you can), that the noun functions as a subject (nominative case from the Latin word for name) or an object (objective case). In any case (pardon the pun) the form of a noun remains the same regardless of how it is used. The personal pronoun, however changes form depending on its use.

The following list is for the **nominative case** (personal pronoun used as a subject).

> **First person** refers to the speaker or speakers
> > singular *I*, plural *we*
>
> *I* **am going to the party.** *I* is the subject, the thing we're talking about.
>
> *We* **are going to the party, if you have money for gas.** *We* is the subject.
>
> **Second person** refers to the person or persons spoken to
> > singular *you*, plural *you*
>
> *You* **are going to the party.** *You* is the subject.
>
> **Are all of *you* going without me?** You is the subject. *All of you* indicates more than one person; *you* can be used alone, but the reference to more than one person is not as clear.

Third person refers to the person(s) or thing(s) spoken of
    singular *he, she* or *it*, plural *they*

He **is going to the party.** *He* is the subject.

She **is going with him.** Now *she* it is the subject.

It **sounds like a great party.** *It* is the subject, standing in for
party. The sentence could be reconstructed to say *The party
sounds great.* or *The party, it sounds great.*

They **are not taking me with them.** *They* is the subject.

The personal pronoun as an object (objective case) often gets us into trouble,
because we use it in the wrong place.

The list which follows is for the **objective case**.

    First person (speaker)
        singular *me*, plural *us*

Will you take *me* **to the party?** *Me* is the object of the verb *take*.

Please join *us* **at the party.** *Us* is the object of the verb *join*. (*You*
is the implied subject as in *Will you join us at the party?*)

    Second person (spoken to)
        singular *you*, plural *you*

We will be happy to join *you*. *You* is the object of the verb *join*.

We will be happy to join all of *you*. *You* is the object of the verb
join. Here, again, *you* can be used alone (and probably would
be) to imply a group.

    Third person (spoken of)
        singular *him, her* or *it*, plural *them*

Let us join *him*. *Him* is the object of the verb *join*.

Let us join *her*. *Her* is the object of the verb *join*.

We will take *it* **home with us.** *It* is the object of the verb *take*.

Let's take *them* **home too.** *Them* is the object of the verb *take*.

The personal pronoun at the beginning of a sentence doesn't seem to give us any difficulty. Nor does the personal pronoun as an object.

So what's the problem? It's a thing called the **predicate pronoun**. When a pronoun refers back to a noun or pronoun which is the subject (nominative) it too must remain nominative.

> **It is *she* who called.**
>
> **It is *her* who called?**
>
> Which is it?
>
>> Stop! Look the sentence over. The order of the sentence is getting us into trouble. *It* is standing in for *she*; you might consider *it* an anchor to hold down the beginning of the sentence (called an **expletive**) when the rest of the sentence is out of order. You can get out of trouble by analyzing the sentence as it is or you can correct the order as long as you are careful not to change the meaning.
>
> **It is *she*.**
>
> **It is *her*.**
>
>> *It is she* sounds the same to most people as *it is her*. Come on, admit it. When your favorite singer steps out on stage what do you say? "It's her!" But now try. . .
>
> ***She* is who called. *She* is the one who called.**
>
> ***Her* is who. . .** uh, oh.
>
>> *She is (the one) who called* compared to *her is (the one) who called* certainly makes it clear. So it is *she* who called. Your ears will lie to you if given a chance, especially if you've been hearing something wrong for most of your life.
>
>> Try changing the order of the words when in doubt . . . or adding words. Does *it is we* (or *they*) sound wrong to you? Flesh out the sentence.
>
> **It is *we* (who are the ones) who did something.**
>
> ***We* did something.** It is *we*, for sure.

Again, before we move on: if correct grammar doesn't sound right to you, doesn't feel right to you or sounds affected, don't use it. Get rid of the awkward construction and express yourself in another way.

This seems like a good place to mention **who and whom.** Please don't cringe. It's easy.

> **Who is nominative** (a subject), single and plural.

> **Whom is objective** (an object), single and plural.

It is she who called.

> *Who* refers to *she* which we already decided is nominative (see above). But *whom* did she call?

> If this one gives you a problem, change the order of the words.

She called whom?

> Still doesn't sound right? Substitute another word.

She called me?

> *Me* is objective (see above) therefore you need the objective case of *who* which is *whom*. Again, if you don't like the way it sounds, when properly phrased, figure out another way to say it.

The **possessive case** of the personal pronoun also changes form depending on how it is being used. Often the possessive case is used as an adjective to modify a noun. To complicate matters, there are several possessives which have two forms (don't give up now), one of which is always used to modify a noun and one which is always used alone, as a pronoun. It's easiest to deal with if you always think of the possessive as a modifier.

A selection of simple sentences to illustrate the use of possessive person pronouns seems preferable to quoting a lot of rules. Hope you agree.

> **First person possessive** (speaker)
> singular — *my* or *mine*

> *My* **car has a dented fender.** *My* is used as an adjective to modify *car* by indicating ownership

44

The car with the dented fender is *mine*. *Mine* is a pronoun taking the place of *car* or more precisely, *my car*. The sentence could be rephrased as **The car with the dented fender is *my* car.** or *My car* **is the car with the dented fender.** Sorry to belabor that; just want to show how reconstructing the sentence can help clarify exactly what the word represents.

My **cars are here. The cars are *mine*.** Here you can see that changing the number of the noun which is being modified or replaced does not change the number or form of the possessive pronoun as long as the ownership is still in the hands of one person, me. Thus shall it ever be with modifiers; consider **the *brown* cow** versus **the *brown* cows** and **the cow is *brown*** versus **the cows are *brown*** (not *browns*, unless they belong to the Browns, but that's another story).

First person possessive (speaker)
    plural — *our* or *ours*

Our **car is a rust bucket.** *Our* modifies car, and is plural which indicates possession by more than one person.

This rust bucket is *ours*. *Ours* takes the place of *rust bucket*. **Ours is the rust bucket.**

Our **cars are here. These cars are *ours*.** Again, no change in the modifier even though the number of the noun modified changes.

Second person (spoken to)
    singular and plural are the same —*your* or *yours*

Your **child isn't doing well in school.** *Your* modifies the noun *child*. The form is the same for the single or plural *you*, whether it is one spouse addressing another or a teacher addressing both parents.

The child with the glazed look is *yours*. (Yeah, sure.) *Yours* stands in for *your child* whether addressing one parent or both.

Your **children are here. The children are *yours*.** Whether one child or many the personal pronoun is the same.

Third person (spoken of)
   singular — *his, her* or *hers, its*

His **violin is on stage. The green case is *his*.** In the first sentence, *his* modifies *violin*; in the second, *green case* is replaced by the pronoun *his*. In both instances the pronoun takes the same form.

Her **banjo is in the car. The five-string banjo is *hers*.** In the first sentence, *her* modifies *banjo*; in the second, *five-string banjo* is replaced by the pronoun *hers*. In each case, the form is different. Why does *her* change form while *his* does not? Like so many of the anomalies in English, nobody knows.

Its **stall is in the barn.** *Its* modifies stall. Examples of the use of *its* (a possessive form, remember) without a noun seem to be restricted to poetry or grammarians who are stretching a point to make a point and serve more to confuse than enlighten. If you should find an example you like, write it in here.

Third person (spoken of)
   plural — *their* or *theirs*

Their **zither is in the case.** *Their* modifies *zither*.

The zither in the case is *theirs*. *Theirs* replaces *zither*.

Their **zithers are in the case. The zithers in the case are *theirs*.** And finally, multiple zithers retain the same pronoun.

Whose is the possessive form of *who*. It is the same whether singular or plural, nominative or objective. Whose idea was it to make something so easy?

   Whose car is this? This car is whose?

   Whose cars are these? These cars are whose?

Attack of the like sounding words

There are words which sound like personal pronouns but have entirely different meanings. You are not likely to use *hours* for *ours*, *ewe* for *you* or *hymn* for *him*. In fact, we both know that you're not likely to make any of the mistakes mentioned in this book, but there are others who might and you should be aware of them.

To be sure that the words you write are saying what you mean, remember that the personal pronoun never takes an apostrophe to form the possessive, then redo the sentence using the complete words that make up any contractions you have used.

Its is the possessive form for *it*.
> **Its cage is clean.** (No apostrophe, so it is possessive.)

It's is the contraction of *it is*.
> **It's a clean cage.** (*It is* a clean cage. It works!)

Their is the possessive form for *they*.
> **Their cage is clean.**

They're is the contraction of *they are*.
> **They're in a clean cage.**

Whose is the possessive form for *who* or *whom*.
> **Whose cage is this?**

Who's is the contraction of *who is*.
> **Who's in this cage?**

Your is the possessive form for *you*.
> **Your cage is ready.**

You're is the contraction of *you are*.
> **You're in the wrong cage.**

Got it? Now just keep your cage clean.

Indefinite pronouns

Indefinite pronouns are those which name things in a general way. Most indefinite pronouns express quantity, however imprecise.

Some of the commonly used indefinite pronouns:

all	**another**	**any**	**anybody**
anyone	**both**	**each**	**either**
everybody	**everyone**	**everything**	**few**
many	**most**	**neither**	**nobody**
none	**nothing**	**one**	**other**
several	**some**	**somebody**	**someone**
something	**somewhat**		

Certain pronoun phrases are also viewed as indefinite pronouns:

any one	**every one**	**each other**	**no one**
one another	**some one**		

If you are paying attention, you will have noticed that some words are on both of the above lists, first as a compound word, then as two separate words. Often the only difference is spelling; the words mean the same whichever form is used. Sometimes, a difference in structure can create a different shade of meaning and you may want to take advantage of it.

Someone will be held responsible. Refers to anyone, anywhere and perhaps more than one.

Some one of us (of you, of management) will be held responsible. Narrows the field and implies only one.

The phrases **one another** and **each other** deserve mention. *One another* refers to the action of more than two whereas *each other* refers to only two.

Love one another, like the song says, unless you are speaking of that special someone, in which case **you love each other.**

This is one of those preferences mentioned earlier in which there is no absolute right and wrong. Either way you say it will be understood, so if you

48

disagree with the suggestion, love in the way which you find most comfortable.

As stated above, indefinite pronouns generally imply imprecise numbers, but you shouldn't be imprecise in the use of the terms.

> **Everybody wants to go. Nobody likes it.** We have a tendency to voice the extreme even when its not exactly true.

> **Almost everyone wants to go. Few like it. Most do not like it.** Using a modifier or a different word results in a statement that is still imprecise, but properly so, rather than a statement which is precisely incorrect.

Casual use of indefinite pronouns may be normal, accepted and even understood within your normal sphere of influence, but it can trivialize your message in some circles and reflect on your competence. Get in the habit of being as precise as you can all of the time and you will be precise when it is most important.

How many is a few? An insignificant amount, according to the dictionary. Some people claim that a few means three. It all depends on your frame of reference. If you have a million fruit flies and a few get away, a few could be a thousand. Twenty complaints about a product you sell could be described as few if you sold 20,000. It's all relative — just be sure that you and the receiver of your message are of like mind.

The **possessive form of the indefinite pronoun** is usually shown by adding apostrophe s, because, unlike the personal pronoun, there is no special form to show possession and the indefinite pronoun is usually used only in the singular (The word is singular even though its meaning implies plurality)

anybody's stuff	**anyone's stuff**	**everybody's stuff**
everyone's stuff	**nobody's stuff**	**one's stuff**
somebody's stuff	**someone's stuff**	

One exception is *other* which forms a plural by adding *s* and so takes an apostrophe after the *s* to show the plural possessive.

> **my *other* stuff** —singular only

> **put it with the *others*** —plural only

> **put it with the *others'* stuff** —plural possessive

49

An oddity in English is the association of the adverb *else* with an indefinite pronoun.

anyone else   **everyone else**   **no one else**

someone else

When forming the possessive of the pronoun, *else* is treated as though it is part of the word and takes an apostrophe *s*.

anyone else's   **everyone else's**   **no one else's**

someone else's

Relative pronouns

The relative pronoun is a bridge which connects its antecedent (the noun to which it refers) to a new clause. It is particularly useful in avoiding clumsy construction when you have one clause imbedding in another.

A man *who* was a member of the group returned the next day.
The pronoun *who* takes the place of man and forms a bridge between *man* and *member of the group.* It may be better understood if you consider the alternatives.

Two sentences — **The man was a member of the group. He returned the next day.**

A parenthetical phrase — **The man (he was part of the group) returned the next day.**

This violin, *which* she has been playing for years, is her most treasured possession. *Which* takes the place of *violin* and is the bridge between violin (Is that another pun? Shame.) and *she has been playing for years.* Again, consider the alternatives.

She has been playing this violin for years. It is her most treasured possession.

This violin (she has been playing it for years) is her most treasured possession.

Nothing wrong with the two sentences or the parenthetical phrase in the sentence, but there are times when you will want to vary the pace of your writing and this is one of the ways in which you can do it.

The relative pronouns *who, whom* or *whose* refer to a person, *what* or *which* refer to anything except a person and *that* refers to anything.

What requires some special consideration. It replaces *that which* and so should not be used where the antecedent is expressed.

> **This violin,** *what* **she has been...** don't sound good; nor do **This violin,** *that which* **she has been...** because the antecedent *violin* has been expressed and *what* or *that which* just don't fit. *Which* is correct — **This violin,** *which* **she has been...**

> **Do** *what* **you will to murder this language.** — a nasty sentiment, but grammatically correct.

That doesn't *require* special consideration, but does deserve it. For one thing, it finds a lot of work as a demonstrative pronoun (see below). For another, it exhibits a harsh, flat sound in contrast to *who* and *which,* and thus seems out of place in some situations where it is grammatically correct.

> **The lady,** *whom* **I have just met,....** — is not likely to be described in the same tone as — **The scoundrel** *that* **stole my watch....**

Recognize that this is one of those personal preference things; consider your style, decide what sounds best to you and use it.

Other part-time relative pronouns are **but** and **such as**.

> **There,** *but* **for the grace of God, go I.**

> **My life,** *such as* **it is, is quite pleasant.**

Interrogative pronouns

> **An interrogative pronoun is one which introduces a question.**

Who or *whom* refers to a person.

> *Who* **chased the cat?**

> **To** *whom* **did you give the cat?**

Whose (possessive) generally refers to a person.

> *Whose* cat is this? *Whose* refers to a person — literally, **What person owns** this cat?

What and *which* refer to anything.

> **What** is this? Response depends on the nature of the creature or thing indicated; most likely a name or description.

> **What** is she? The question *Who is she?* is generally seeking a name and perhaps a common reference such as to whom the person in question is related or her position in the community. *What is she?* is more likely related to a conversation about occupation, religious preference, nationality, etc.

> **Which** car is yours? *Which* of you chased the cat?

Demonstrative pronouns

The demonstrative pronouns are *this* (*plural these*) and *that*(*plural those*); *demonstrative* from the Latin, *to point out*, they literally or figuratively point out the proximity of the noun which they represent.

> *This* is my coat and *that* is my hat. *This* indicates a coat near at hand, whereas the hat is further away.

> *These* people have shelter; what can be done about *those* who have none? *These people* points to a specific group; *those*, with no antecedent, figuratively points to a group, out there, somewhere.

Had enough of pronouns? If not, browse through another text where you will probably find a class of pronouns not mentioned in this book, just as some described here are not on other lists. Weren't you warned that this is an inexact science and that there is no definitive text? That any book of grammar you choose will reflect in some way the predilections of the author or compiler? It means that you will have to think for yourself and make some judgments only you can make if you really want to use the language well.

Enough, already! Let's move on to **the action**.

Verbs — the action

Verbs are where the action is. A verb can initiate a thought expression in a one-word sentence.

> Go! Come! Hurry! Drive! Dig! Smell! Eat! Smile! Enter! Drink! Ready! Aim! Fire!

Function of the verb

The function of a verb is to indicate action or a state of being, usually with reference to time and condition of the action or state of being.

Don't panic! We can break that definition down to manageable chunks.

action — The verb tells you that *something is being done,* that some action is taking place. In all probability, you're familiar with this one. - Joe *drives* the car. Sue *slaps* the smart-aleck writer.

state of being — You might think of the verb as indicating a state of being when it's not describing an action. Joe *is* nervous. Sue *appears* contented. These are called *linking verbs* because they forge a link between the subject and a word describing the condition or state of being of the subject. For a more thorough discussion, see **Linking verbs,** below.

time and condition — The verb indicates *when the action takes place* (in the past, at present, in the future) and the *condition of the action,* (completed, in progress, not started) by its form. See **Forms of the verb,** below.

Forms of the verb

There is no way to ease into this gently, so let's just dive in and define all of those pesky forms, or at least the ones which seem important at the moment; we can elaborate on their idiosyncrasies later.

The infinitive — The infinitive might be considered the unadulterated form of a verb, one which is expressed without the limits of person or number imposed by attachment to a noun. The infinitive (think *infinity*, unlimited) covers an indefinite span of time and conditions.

It is better *to give* than to wash your socks.

See **Infinitives**, page 56.

Present tense — Also referred to as the *present indicative* (See **Mood**, below). The *present* form of a verb alludes to the time of the statement in which it appears.

She *speaks* as though she will never stop.

We might rephrase the sentence.

Whenever she *speaks*, it is as though she will never stop.

The reference is not to past or future, but to *that time when she speaks*.

Present participle — The present participle is a verb form which may also function as an adjective to describe a present action which is not completed.

The politician, *speaking* about his accomplishments, never seemed to take a breath.

The present participle form always ends in *-ing*.

Present progressive — The *present progressive* form differs little from the present participle. It describes a continuous action and is formed by joining a form of the verb *to be* to the present participle.

He *is speaking* as though he will never stop.

Present perfect — Also referred to as the *present perfect tense*. The *present perfect* defines an action which has just been completed. It is formed by using *have* or *has* with the *past participle* form of the verb.

He *has spoken* and is ready to take questions.

Past tense — Also called *past indicative*, the past tense indicates action, or a state of being that existed, in the past.

She spoke to the group last year.

Past participle — The past participle suggests an action which, though completed, is continuing.

Every place she went they heard her words *spoken* with pride.

Past progressive — The past progressive form differs little from the past participle. It describes a continuous action and is formed by joining a form of the verb *to be* to the present participle.

Every place she went, she *was speaking* with pride the words she wrote.

Past perfect — Also referred to as *past perfect tense*, the past perfect is formed by using *had* with the past participle of the verb. It indicates a past action which was completed prior to another event in the past.

He *had spoken* before the last meeting.

Future tense — The future tense makes a declaration about action to be taken or a condition anticipated in the future. The future tense is formed by using *shall* or *will* with the verb.

He *will speak* at the next meeting.

Future progressive — The future progressive describes a continuous action in the future and is formed by joining a form of the verb *to be* to the present participle.

They *shall be speaking* the words she wrote.

Future perfect — Also described as *future perfect tense*, the future perfect is formed by adding *shall have* or *will have* to the past participle of the verb to indicate an action whose completion is anticipated before another future event.

He *will have spoken* to the group twice after the next meeting.

The gerund — The gerund is a verb form, specifically the present participle, used as a noun. It is mentioned briefly in the section on **Nouns** and is of no more importance here than it was there.

Our obsession with cataloguing and relegating everything to nice neat slots has its merits, but sometimes it gets us into trouble. Especially when something doesn't fit into those nice neat slots and those doing the cataloguing can't agree where the misfit belongs. Thus far we've gone through a list of the more popular terms used to classify verbs which are, without doubt, the most difficult of the parts of speech to comprehend, probably because they are the most versatile. In any event this is the base on which we will build as we explore the use of verbs and other parts of speech in the rest of this section and sentence structure in the next.

The attempts to organize English have resulted in some loose fits for words, so don't be surprised by ambiguity, overlapping and downright disagreement from one text to another and even within a single text. The alternative is a static language which wouldn't be nearly as much fun.

Linking verbs

All verbs do not express action. A verb which expresses a state of being rather than the action of a noun is called a *linking verb* because its function is to connect the subject with another noun, a pronoun or an adjective which describes it. The most common *linking verbs* are the forms of **to be**:

be	was	been	am
is	are	were	shall be
will be	shall have been		will have been
had been	may be	may have been	
might be	might have been		being

Other *linking verbs* are:

appear	become	feel	grow
look	hear	keep	prove
seem	smell	sound	stay
taste	turn	remain	

Become and seem are almost always linking verbs. The other verbs in the list above may be either *linking* or *action* depending on how they are used.

> **The outside air *is* cold.** The linking verb always requires the word or phrase which complements the noun. **The outside air is.** means nothing (unless you are a student of Zen – then it's like the sound of one hand clapping).

> **The flowers *smell* fragrant.** *Smell* is used as a linking verb. In this example, if you leave off the complement, the sentence takes on an entirely different meaning.

Usually, the linking verb can be replaced by a form of *seem*, a good test if you want to determine the verb's function .

Auxiliary verbs

Until now, we've referred to verbs as a single word. That's only part of the story. The verb may, in fact, be a *verb phrase* made up of two or more words. In such cases, the last word in the *verb phrase*, the verb which indicates the action, is the *principal verb* and those which precede it are helpers or *auxiliary verbs*.

> **The students *study* in the library.**

> **The students *are studying* in the dorms.**

> **The students *should have been studying* in the classroom.**

> **The students *had better study* somewhere!**

Some of the more common auxiliary verbs are:

am	are	can	could	could be
could have been	did	do	does	
had	had been	had better	had rather	has
has been	have	have been	is	may
might	must	must have	must have been	
shall	shall be	should	should have	
should have been	was	were	will	
will be	would	would have		

57

Infinitives — split and otherwise

The word *to* is a preposition; however, when it precedes a verb, it is considered to be part of an infinitive. The infinitive is, then, a *verb* preceded by the word *to*.

He has a desire *to write* well.

To run in the marathon is her goal.

(Her goal *is to run* in the marathon.)

Sounds too simple, and it is. When auxiliaries such as **can, could, do, may, might, must, shall, should, will, would, had better** and **had rather** are used, the auxiliary phrase often replaces the word *to* in order to avoid awkward construction.

He felt that anyone with the ability *should write*.

(He felt that anyone with the ability *to write should do so*.)

Use of *to* is optional after some words such as:

bid	dare	help	let
make	need	please	see

Don't you dare (to) smoke in here!

Now for those nasty **split infinitives**. No big deal! There is a school of thought which dictates that modifiers should never be placed between *to* and its verb, thereby splitting the infinitive.

She has one wish, *to sing sweetly*.
versus
She has one wish, *to sweetly sing*. (split infinitive)

To run swiftly was his goal.
versus
To swiftly run was his goal. (split infinitive)

Test it out on any sentence of your choosing and you will likely find that the split infinitive doesn't distort meaning, but it is a bit awkward. *However*, there are times when the construction fits the mood of the message and *when that happens, use it!* NEXT!

Basic Grammar — Putting It All Together

Inflection

Inflection refers to the pattern of changes in words which properly express grammatical relationships such as case, number, gender, person, tense, etc. In verbs these are called **conjugation.** (See **Tense**, below.)

Tense

Tense? Indeed! Verbs always make us tense. But that's not what we need to discuss here.

As stated above, a verb indicates a time when the action takes place. The form of the verb which relates it to time is its **tense: past, present or future.** It is important to be familiar with these forms in order to convey a message that is not confusing.

The modified forms of the verb should be included in any listing of tense because they convey different shades of meaning.

present	past	future
present participle	past participle	
present progressive	past progressive	future progressive
present perfect	past perfect	future perfect

The general rule regarding tense is not to change within a sentence. The tense of a subordinate clause should agree with the tense of the main verb. Not as easy as it sounds, nor does it apply universally.

> **He** *wants* **to drive**, for example, in an indirect reference becomes **She** *said* **that he** *wanted* **to drive** changing *want* from the present tense to the past tense in order to force agreement with *said*, which is past tense. In this instance, you might view the rule as superfluous, because **She** *said* **that he** *wants* **to drive** loses nothing in translation. You would be right; however, there are times when the message will be unclear if there is not agreement in tense.

It is better to use the correct form so that you are sure that the communication will always be clear.

If the action expressed is continual, future or universal, the present tense may be retained in the subordinate clause.

She *said* **that he always** *wants* **to drive.**

She *said* **that he will always** *want* **to drive.**

She *said* **that he still** *wants* **to drive.**

The present tense may be retained in the subordinate clause for emphasis.

She *said* **that he** *is* **driving.**

If the clauses are independent, the tense need not agree.

If he *said* **that, I** *can't* **stop him.** Reiterating that which happened in the past is independent of the present action.

More of this in the sections on **Sentence structure** and **Relationships**. Just don't get tense about tense. (Isn't English fun?)

Regular verbs form the past tense and past participle by adding -*ed* to the verb. When the verb ends in a silent *e*, the *e* is not repeated; add only -*d*. Irregular verbs form the past tense and past participle in a variety of ways; there is no single rule governing their conjugation. The most commonly used irregular verbs are listed in the next section.

Rules for conjugating other forms of the verbs are contained in the section, **Forms of the verb**, above.

Irregular verbs

There is no way to identify and conjugate irregular verbs except to know which verbs are irregular or to look them up. You probably already know most from regular use and the list which begins on the next page will help.

In addition to the irregular verbs with their irregular conjugation, some of the regular verbs have alternative forms; those which are in general use have been included. The regular verbs on this list are easily recognized because they show two forms, one of which follows the rule for adding -*ed*.

This is not a complete list of the irregular verbs for English. Verbs and verb forms which are not in common use have been omitted as well as any in common use which we may have overlooked.

Principal parts of irregular verbs

Present	Past	Past Participle
arise	arose	arisen
awake	awoke	awoke
	awaked	awaked
be	was	been
bear	bore	borne
beat	beat	beat
		beaten
become	became	become
befall	befell	befallen
begin	began	begun
behold	beheld	beheld
bend	bent	bent
	bended	bended
bereave	bereft	bereft
	bereaved	bereaved
beseech	besought	besought
bet	bet	bet
	betted	betted
bid	bid	bid
	bade	bidden
bind	bound	bound
bite	bit	bitten
bleed	bled	bled
bless	blest	blest
	blessed	blessed
blow	blew	blown
break	broke	broken
breed	bred	bred
bring	brought	brought
build	built	built
burn	burnt	burnt
	burned	burned
burst	burst	burst
buy	bought	bought
can	could	

61

Principal parts of irregular verbs (continued)

Present	Past	Past Participle
cast	cast	cast
catch	caught	caught
choose	chose	chosen
cling	clung	clung
clothe	clad	clad
	clothed	clothed
come	came	come
cost	cost	cost
creep	crept	crept
cut	cut	cut
deal	dealt	dealt
dig	dug	dug
do	did	done
draw	drew	drawn
dream	dreamt	dreamt
	dreamed	dreamed
drink	drank	drunk
		drunken
drive	drove	driven
dwell	dwelt	dwelt
	dwelled	dwelled
eat	ate	eaten
fall	fell	fallen
feed	fed	fed
feel	felt	felt
fight	fought	fought
find	found	found
flee	fled	fled
fling	flung	flung
fly	flew	flown
forbear	forbore	forborne
forbid	forbade	forbidden
forget	forgot	forgotten
forsake	forsook	forsaken

Principal parts of irregular verbs (continued)

Present	Past	Past Participle
freeze	froze	frozen
get	got	gotten
		got
give	gave	given
go	went	gone
grind	ground	ground
grow	grew	grown
hang	hung	hung
	hanged	hanged
have	had	had
hear	heard	heard
hew	hewed	hewn
hide	hid	hidden
hit	hit	hit
hold	held	held
hurt	hurt	hurt
keep	kept	kept
kneel	knelt	knelt
	kneeled	kneeled
know	knew	known
lay	laid	laid
lead	led	led
leap	leapt	leapt
	leaped	leaped
leave	left	left
lend	lent	lent
let	let	let
lie	lay	lain
light	lit	lit
	lighted	lighted
lose	lost	lost
make	made	made
may	might	

Principal parts of irregular verbs (continued)

Present	Past	Past Participle
mean	meant	meant
meet	met	met
mow	mowed	mown
pay	paid	paid
plead	plead	plead
put	put	put
quit	quit	quit
	quitted	quitted
read	read	read
rend	rent	rent
rid	rid	rid
ride	rode	ridden
ring	rang	rung
	rung	
rise	rose	risen
run	ran	run
say	said	said
see	saw	seen
seek	sought	sought
sell	sold	sold
send	sent	sent
set	set	set
sew	sewed	sewn
		sewed
shake	shook	shaken
shall	should	
shave	shaved	shaven
		shaved
shed	shed	shed
shine	shone	shone
	shined	shined
shoe	shod	shod
shoot	shot	shot
show	showed	shown, showed

Principal parts of irregular verbs (continued)

Present	Past	Past Participle
shred	shred	shred
	shredded	shredded
shrink	shrank	shrunk
	shrunk	shrunken
shut	shut	shut
sing	sang	sung
sink	sank	sunk
	sunk	
sit	sat	sat
slay	slew	slain
slide	slid	slid
		slidden
sling	slung	slung
slit	slit	slit
sow	sowed	sown
speak	spoke	spoken
speed	sped	sped
spend	spent	spent
split	split	split
spread	spread	spread
spring	sprang	sprung
	sprung	
stand	stood	stood
steal	stole	stolen
stick	stuck	stuck
sting	stung	stung
stink	stank	stunk
	stunk	
strew	strewed	strewn
		strewed
stride	strode	stridden
strike	struck	stricken
		struck
strive	strove	striven
swear	swore	sworn
sweat	sweat	sweat
	sweated	sweated

Principal parts of irregular verbs (continued)

Present	Past	Past Participle
sweep	swept	swept
swell	swelled	swollen
		swelled
swim	swam	swum
	swum	
swing	swung	swung
take	took	taken
teach	taught	taught
tear	tore	torn
tell	told	told
think	thought	thought
throw	threw	thrown
thrust	thrust	thrust
tread	trod	trodden
		trod
wake	woke	waked
	waked	
wear	wore	worn
wed	wed	wed
	wedded	wedded
weep	wept	wept
wet	wet	wet
	wetted	wetted
will	would	
win	won	won
wind	wound	wound
wring	wrung	wrung
write	wrote	written

Transitive and intransigent verbs

This is another one of those items that doesn't crop up often in polite conversation, but you may want to know about it just in case it comes up in the next section.

Verbs are classified as transitive or intransitive based on their relation to objects. **Transitive** describes a verb which requires an object to make the meaning of a sentence complete; an **intransitive** verb does not require an object. Many verbs may be used either way, depending on the sentence

> **The boy *reads* the *book* well.** *Reads* in this sentence is transitive; *book* is the object and we need to know that to make this particular thought complete.

> **The girl *reads* well.** *Reads* in this sentence is intransitive; the lack of an object makes it clear that this is a general comment about the girl's ability to read

Now, aren't you glad you know that?

Incidentally, *intransigent* means unable to compromise; rebellious — sounds like a lot of the verbs we've seen so far.

Mood, voice, person and number

So far we've looked at the ability of the verb to indicate time (**forms of the verb, tense**) and we've looked at some of the types of verbs (**linking verbs, auxiliary verbs, infinitives, regular verbs, irregular verbs**). Now we'll look at some of the other properties of verbs.

Mood is the manner in which the action or condition expressed by the verb is stated, whether actual (**indicative**), doubtful (**subjunctive**) or commanding (**imperative**). Yes, you might as well learn the names, because they could come up again.

> **Indicative** — Think of *indicate*, to point out or direct attention to, a positive action. The indicative mood is a statement of fact or a question of fact.

> **This is my house, the only brick one on the block.**

> **Where is your book?**   **I like to dance.**

Subjunctive — The word is from the Latin for subjoin, which is dumb. If you want to remember it coupled with what it describes, think of *submissive*. The subjunctive mood expresses a contingency, a supposition or desire. The statement is usually introduced by a conjunction of doubt, contingency, condition or possibility such as *if, though, unless* or *whether*.

If this *were* my house I'd have it painted.

I wish this *were* my book.

May I *have* this dance? (I wonder *if* I may have this dance?)

Imperative — The imperative mood expresses command, entreaty or exhortation. *Imperative* means obligatory which makes this one easy to remember.

Come with me to the house. **Read the book.**

Watch the dance and see how it flows.

Voice refers to the form of a *transitive verb* that indicates whether the subject is performing the action (**active**) or is being acted upon (**passive**).

Active — **She wrote the play.** The action *wrote* was performed by the subject *she*.

Passive — **The play was written by her.** The action *written* was performed on the subject *play*.

Person of the action described by a verb is the same as for the pronoun:

First person — the person or persons speaking.

Second person — the person or persons spoken to.

Third person — the person or persons spoken of.

This might be a good time to review persons as outlined in the section on **Pronouns.** You've probably forgotten it by now and we can wait. . . .

Number in grammar refers to the singular and plural forms of a word. The bad news is that verbs have singular and plural forms which must agree with the number of the noun or pronoun. The good news is that except for *to be*, the verb changes form *only* in the third person singular.

Basic Grammar — Putting It All Together

To be or not to be, that is maddening

To be is the weirdest verb we have. Naturally it's also the most useful and you can't ignore it. It has been written that the only way to learn the forms of *to be* is to memorize them. The writer obviously never hear of crib sheets. Here's yours with *to be* and the regular verb *call* together for comparison. Admittedly there is a great deal of redundancy because the forms don't change as much as you might imagine, but how can you know without seeing it? The verb forms are in **bold face** with helpers in *italics*.

	first person (speaking)	second person (spoken to)	third person (spoken of)
Present tense			
singular—to be	I **am**	you **are**	he, she, it **is**
singular—call	I **call**	you **call**	he, she, it **calls** (This is the only verb change which relates to number—third person singular.)
plural—to be	we **are**	you **are**	they **are**
plural—call	we **call**	you **call**	they **call**
Present perfect			
singular—to be	I *have* **been**	you *have* **been**	he, she, it *has* **been**
singular—call	I *have* **called**	you *have* **called**	he, she, it *has* **called** (Note that the rule was followed for forming the *present perfect* by using *have* with the *past participle* which in turn had been formed by adding *-ed* to the verb. To find the past participle of an irregular verb refer to the list of irregular verbs above.)
plural—to be	we *have* **been**	you *have* **been**	they *have* **been**
plural—call	we *have* **called**	you *have* **called**	they *have* **called**

69

Past tense

singular—to be	I **was**	you **were**	he, she, it **was**
singular—call	I **called**	you **called**	he, she, it **called**
plural—to be	we **were**	you **were**	they **were**
plural—call	we **called**	you **called**	they **called**

Past perfect

singular—to be	I *had* **been**	you *had* **been**	he, she, it *had* **been**
singular—call	I *had* **called**	you *had* **called**	he, she, it *had* **called**

(The past perfect is formed by using had with the past participle.)

plural—to be	we *had* **been**	you *had* **been**	they *had* **been**
plural—call	we *had* **called**	you *had* **called**	they *had* **called**

Future tense

singular—to be	I *shall* **be**	you *will* **be**	he, she, it *will* **be**
singular—call	I *shall* **call**	you *will* **call**	he, she, it *will* **call**
plural—to be	we *shall* **be**	you *will* **be**	they *will* **be**
plural—call	we *shall* **call**	you *will* **call**	they *will* **call**

Future perfect

singular—to be	I *shall have* **been**	you *will have* **been**	he, she, it *will have* **been**
singular—call	I *shall have* **called**	you *will have* **called**	he, she, it *will have* **called**

(The future perfect is formed by adding *shall have* or *will have* to the past participle)

plural—to be	we *shall have* **been**	you *will have* **been**	they *will have* **been**
plural—call	we *shall have* **called**	you *will have* **called**	they *will have* **called**

Those nasty dangling participles

Better to split an infinitive than to dangle a participle. No joke. The split infinitive may sound awkward; the dangling participle can be downright confusing. The *participial phrase,* made up of the participle and its modifiers, is in turn modifying a noun. A *dangling participle* is one which was left hanging out there somewhere with no obvious attachment to the thing it is supposed to modify.

> **Walking through the woods, there were animals everywhere.** Can't you just see it? Raccoons, bears and foxes strolling hand in hand in their Sunday best.

> **Walking through the woods, we could see there were animals everywhere.** Sounds better. There are many ways to frame this sentence, none of which allow you to drop the *we* to which the participial phrase refers.

Sometimes the error is so subtle that it is hardly noticed.

> **Opening the door, the room seemed very large.** Okay, so you realize that the room didn't open the door and you change the sentence. **Opening the door, *we* could see that the room seemed very large.**

> **Looking through the window, the room seemed very large.** You could walk by this one all day without flinching. You might rationalize that you are dealing with a few unvoiced words and take the sentence to mean exactly what it does mean. ***We were* looking through the window, *and* the room seemed very large.** Sorry, but you can't (or rather, shouldn't) do it. It is only by chance that the meaning of the sentence does not appear to be confused by the dangling participle. Depending on the context, that is, what is said before and after this sentence, it's meaning may yet be in question.

Effective communication should clarify, not confuse and the dangling participle will almost always serve to confuse.

Odds and ends

Characteristic of a vital growing language, English is rife with idiosyncrasies which defy categorizing. Following are a few, though certainly not all, of the anomalies of the verb family.

Had ought is one of those phrases that should make you cringe. *Ought* means *should*, though it is more emphatic, implying a greater sense of obligation.

> You *should* **do something about that.** The statement engenders the feeling that you might do something if you feel like it.

> You *ought to* **do something about that.** Use of the word ought creates a stronger sense of obligation to do something.

> Use of the word *have* or *had* with *ought* is superfluous. Never mind that it is considered poor form, it doesn't add anything to the message; **You had ought to go** and **I have ought to do it** are old forms which have nothing to recommend them over **You ought to go** and **I ought to do it.**

Had rather and **had better** show up from time to time with mixed results.

I had rather is another old form which has been almost entirely displaced by *I would rather*. Both are correct, so you have only to think about what you are saying and decide which does the job best.

I had better and *you had better* are most frequently used to express the serious nature of the situation.

> **You should go** expresses what you might do if you are so inclined. **You ought to go** expresses a sense of greater obligation. **You had better go** implies that it is likely to get very unfriendly around here if you stay.

Shall and **will** are struggling to be freed from an outdated rule of grammar. To follow this you may want to refer to the crib sheet a few pages back. In the *future tense* you will note that *shall* has been used as an auxiliary in the first person, whereas *will* has been used for the second and third person. *Shall* in the first person expresses *anticipation of a future happening,* whereas *will* does the same in the second and third person. To express *demand or obligation,* the words are reversed; *will* is used for the first person and *shall* for the second and third person.

First person.

(Permissive, anticipation of a future happening.)
I shall wash the car tomorrow. Expresses an anticipated action.

(Directive, a demand or obligation.)
I will wash the car tomorrow. Expresses a determination to act.

Second person.

You will be pleased with the report. Anticipation.

You shall have the report in the morning. Determination.

Third person

She will start work in the morning. Anticipation.

She shall get all the help she needs. Determination.

Observe these distinctions if you want to use the traditional forms.

In contemporary usage, we are more likely to use *shall* and *will* interchangeably, with the emphasis on will as obligatory and shall as pemissive.

Should and **would**, the past tense for *shall* and *will*, may be found under the same dark cloud. *Should* is a synonym for *ought* and although it usually denotes *obligation*, it often indicates *anticipation*. *Would* is usually *permissive*, expressing *desire* or what *might* be expected. They are supposed to follow the same rules as *shall* and *will*, but contemporary usage often dictates quite the opposite.

You shall have the report in the morning expresses determination,
but **You should have the report in the morning** may mean
either *you have a right to expect the report in the morning,* or *if all goes well, I will have it for you in the morning.*

She shall get all the help she needs expresses determination, but
She should get all the help she needs implies *I expect she will get all the help she needs, but I'm not really sure.*

Abbreviating *have* has caused a unique grammatical construction.
Expressions such as *would've, could've* and *might've* strike our ears as *would of, could of* and *might of* which then become committed to writing. Whether writing or speaking, *have* should not be abbreviated in this way. It is just plain sloppy, though of course you can've it your way if you want to.

For a list of words which are often confused, see pages 186-193

For a list of words with dual spellings, see pages 147-148

For a list of irregular verbs, see pages 61-66

For a list of commonly used superfluous words, see page 18

For a list the examples in this book by part of speech, see page 235

Adjectives

Adjectives add color and precision to our speech. Just as the verb gives life to the noun by indicating activity, the adjective gives life to the objects and ideas named by describing them. Adjectives are the words which give us the information to transfer the thing we are talking about from the universal pool of all similar things to a smaller group; perhaps even to a party of one.

Function

The function of an adjective is to clarify what we are talking about by enhancing and limiting the designation of a noun or pronoun.

Articles

The simplest of the adjectives are the articles **a, an,** and **the.** The article is a limiting adjective whose purpose is to point out and limit the noun.

The is the *definite* article and refers to one or more *specific* items.

> **the box** – that box, there

> **the cars in the driveway** – those cars, in that driveway

> **the house on the corner** – that house, located on the corner

The may be used to point out something which is to be further described or something which needs no further description.

A and *an* are the indefinite articles and refer to an unspecified item in a group of items. *A* is used when the noun or modifier which follows it begins with a consonant sound. *An* is used when the noun or modifier is a vowel sound.

> **a box** – any box

> **a car in the driveway** – any car that is in the driveway

> **an artifact from the museum** – any artifact from that museum

> **an outstanding citizen** – any one of the outstanding citizens

Limiting adjectives

Limiting adjectives restrict the nouns which they describe by some reference to number or quantity. Limiting adjectives include the articles listed above, numbers, some of the indefinite pronouns which function as adjectives and adjectives which represent measure or frequency.

three blind mice	a **few** rules
daily newspaper	**double** trouble
both sides of the coin	**every** minute
some fun	**seventy-six** trombones

Numbers are nouns which can function as adjectives and include *cardinal numbers* and *ordinal numbers*. *Cardinal numbers* express a precise amount (one, two, three, four, etc.) *Ordinal numbers* express a relative position (first, second, third, fourth, etc.)

Following is a list of some of the most common limiting adjectives.

a	an	all	any	both
daily	double	each	every	few
half	hourly	inch	many	mile
monthly	most	only	other	second
several	some	the	triple	weekly

Pronouns as adjectives

It seems that at every turn we run into a part of speech masquerading as another part of speech. Sounds complicated, but it really isn't. It's just that it takes a lot of explaining. We've already seen that *indefinite pronouns* can function as adjectives. There are other pronouns which perform this function as well.

The **possessive form of a personal pronoun** may be used as an adjective.

Is *your* friend feeling ill? The pronoun *your* modifies *friend*.

This is *her* computer. The pronoun *her* modifies *computer*.

We like *our* new car. The pronoun *our* modifies *car*.

Demonstrative pronouns (*this, those, that* and *these*) may also function as adjectives. They retain the function of directing attention to or pointing out a noun while they modify the noun by limiting it.

> *This* **car is the one we bought.** *This* points out *car* and modifies, or limits it by singling it out from every other car.

> **I want to see** *those* **books.** *Those* points out **and** modifies *books*.

> **Is** *that* **computer yours?** *That* points out **and** modifies *computer*.

> *These* **grapes are sour.** *These* points out **and** modifies *grapes*.

Descriptive adjectives

The descriptive adjective is one which attributes a non-limiting quality or character to the noun or pronoun.

a *beautiful* child	a *large* bird
a *melodic* song	a *black* sedan
a *charming* play	a *tense* scene
an *exciting* event	a *challenging* puzzle

Comparisons

In addition to ascribing a quality to a noun, the adjective can show the extent to which the attribute applies to a this particular noun in relation to others. There are two degrees of comparison, the *comparative degree* and the *superlative degree* — three if you include the non-comparative form of the adjective, which is silly, because it makes no comparison.

The **comparative degree** is the form of the adjective used for comparing the relationship between two things.

Adjectives of a single syllable usually form the comparative by adding *-er* to the base to indicate a greater degree of the quality expressed.

> **His knife is** *sharper* **than mine.**

> **(Of the two cars) the** *smaller* **is mine.**

> **She keeps a** *neater* **desk than he does.**

Adjectives of more than one syllable are usually preceded by *more* to show a comparison of quality.

> **This perfume is *more fragrant* (than the other one).**

> **The *more beautiful* car is on the left.** (Implying that there is only one car on the right.)

In similar fashion, *less* precedes the adjective to show a lesser degree of the quality.

> **Feeding a gorilla is *less difficult* than giving it a pedicure.**

The **superlative degree** indicates the best of more than two.

Adjectives of a single syllable usually form the superlative by adding -*est* to the base.

> **His is the *sharpest* knife (of all the knives we have).**

> **(Of all the cars) the *smallest* car is mine.**

> **She keeps the *neatest* desk (in the office).**

Adjectives of more than one syllable are usually preceded by most to show the highest degree of the quality compared.

> **This is the *most fragrant* perfume in the store.**

> **She is the *most famous* writer (of all the writers) I know.** (Here's an interesting turn of a phrase. *She* may be the *only* famous writer I know personally, but that's not what I want to say. The form of the sentence implies that I know at least two other writers who might be considered famous, but that may not true. My meaning is that *she is famous and I know her*, and, in spite of the misleading inference, the first sentence is probably the one I will use — but I digress. . .)

Similarly, *least* precedes the adjective to show the lowest degree of the quality compared.

> **The *least difficult* decision to make is to not mess with that gorilla at all.**

We usually add -*er* or -*est* to the adjective of one syllable and use *more* or *most* to precede an adjective of two or more syllables to form comparatives. As you probably expect by now, there are a lot of exceptions. Some follow the basic rules of spelling such as dropping the silent -e , doubling consonants and changing a final y to i before adding -er or -est. A quick look ahead at the section on **Spelling** will help you to spot those.

Adjectives of more than one syllable which are accented on the last syllable may form comparatives by adding -er or -est. Most of these are awkward, however, and you will probably want to use *more* or *most*. Various other adjectives form comparisons in a manner which is contrary to the guidelines or which exhibits no definitive pattern.

The following examples and comments may be of some assistance.

Base	Comparative	Superlative	
bad	worse	worst	—follows no regular pattern
big	bigger	biggest	—adds -er or -est; double consonant spelling rule
clever	cleverer more clever	cleverest most clever	—either form is correct, but *cleverer* seems clumsier
cold	colder	coldest	—regular, adds -er or -est
difficult	more difficult	most difficult	—regular uses *more* or *most*
dry	drier	driest	—adds -er or -est; change -y to i spelling rule
famous	more famous	most famous	—regular, uses *more* or *most*
far	farther further	farthest furthest	—regular, adds -er or -est —no regular pattern (Note: *Farther* or *farthest* is used in the literal sense, to reference distance; *further* or *furthest* is used in the figurative sense, indicating time or degree.)
good	better	best	—no regular pattern
heavy	heavier	heaviest	—adds -er or -est; change -y to i spelling rule
late	later latter	latest last	—adds -er or -est; drop silent -e spelling rule —no regular pattern (Note: *Later* or *latest* is used literally, of time; *latter* or *last* of relative position.)

Base	Comparative	Superlative	(continued)
little	less	least	—no regular pattern

(Note from the font of useless information: Less and least are adjectives as the comparative forms of little. When they are used to modify adjectives, they are adverbs. The same is true for more and most.)

many	more	most	—no regular pattern
much	more	most	—no regular pattern
noble	nobler	noblest	—adds -er or -est; drop silent -e spelling rule
old	elder	eldest	—no regular pattern
	older	oldest	—regular, adds -er or -est

(Note: Elder or eldest denote seniority with the implication of old age; older and oldest imply only the relationship of two or more ages.)

out	outer	outermost	—see **Most**, below
polite	politer	politest	
	more polite	most polite	—either form is correct
pretty	prettier	prettiest	—adds -er or -est; change -y to i spelling rule
sad	sadder	saddest	—adds -er or -est; double consonant spelling rule
severe	severer	severest	—either form is correct, but
	more severe	most severe	*severer* seems awkward
soft	softer	softest	—regular, adds -er or -est
tender	tenderer	tenderest	—*tenderer* seems awkward; how about *more tender*?
wet	wetter	wettest	—adds -er or -est; double consonant spelling rule
willing	more willing	most willing	—regular uses *more* or *most*

Most acts erratically at times and forms the superlative by becoming a suffix to the adjective in words like *hindmost, innermost, outermost* and *uppermost.* Some of the superlatives such as *endmost, foremost* and *topmost* have no comparative degree.

Absolutes and almost absolutes

Not all things can be compared. **Numbers**, for example. If you have three apples, you can't have the most three apples of all those who have three apples. You can however, have the best three apples, but that is a comparison of quality, not quantity. A runner who comes in second can't be any more or less in second place even if there are three other runners who came in second. Second is an absolute position occupied by however many runners placed second. If the runner made a good showing in second place he might be described as having almost come in first.

The are numerous words which by definition do not allow comparison.

alone	blind	dead	empty
entire	eternal	equal	final
full	last	lone	married
mortal	parallel	perfect	premanent
perpetual	perpendicular	round	single
south	square	straight	unique
universal	vertical	whole	wrong

One figure may not be more *square* or *round* than another, two lines may not be more *perpendicular* or *parallel* than two other lines, one love cannot be more *perfect* than another and one person may not be more *dead* than another. They may, however, be *more nearly* square or round or perpendicular or parallel or perfect or dead. The above list is but a small sample of the qualities which cannot be compared. It is important to recognize these qualities in order to be precise in communicating exactly what is meant.

We voice many comparisons and approximations which do not fall into the good, better, best category. (Or good, gooder, goodest, depending on how well you've been following this section.) We speak of arriving *eightish* and staying for the *better part* of an hour, that we ate an *Italian type* meal served *family style*.

Adjectives allow us to form wonderful comparisons which make our expressions more colorful. Do yourself the honor of making proper comparisons so that your audience will listen and enjoy them as much as you do.

Proper adjectives

A proper adjective, which is a proper noun used to describe a characteristic or quality, is generally a product associated with a location or nationality. Note that the proper noun is usually capitalized and the common noun it modifies is not.

Assam tea	*English* muffin
Swiss watch	*Turkish* towel
Irish coffee	*Scottish* tweed
British ale	*Venetian* blinds
Incan artifacts	*Norwegian* sardines
Belfast linen	*Mexican* pottery

Many and few

Customarily, *many* signifies a large number with no special relationship to the total number.

There were *many* people at the fair.

Used with *the,* however, *many* implies a majority and usually refers to people.

The status quo will be changed by the force of the *many.*

In yet another switch, *many a* refers to a large number, but seems to single out individuals.

Many a fool has trod that path. Expressed in this way, the statement has more impact than the simple sentence *Many* **fools have trod that path.**

Few also undergoes a subtle change in meaning when used with an article. Used alone, *few* refers to a small number of random people or things. With the article *a* or *the, few* becomes more selective.

Few are capable of leading. Of *any* total, there are a limited number who are capable.

A few are capable of leading. Of *this* total there are some, perhaps even identified, who are capable.

The people shall be governed by the few. The masses shall be led by a *select* few.

Predicate adjectives

Remember those *linking verbs* we mentioned earlier: all of the forms of *to be,* plus words like *appear, feel, look, seem,* etc.? If you will check your notes, you will find where we said that linking verbs serve to connect the subject with another noun, a pronoun or an adjective. Well, here's the adjective. It's singled out as the *predicate adjective* because it is in the *predicate* (take my word for it; you'll understand when we get to sentence structure), that is, it follows the *verb* although it modifies the *subject,* which appears *before the verb.* Got it?

Don't confuse the predicate adjective with an adjective in the predicate which modifies an object which is not the subject of the sentence.

The grass is *greener* in the well-kept yard. The predicate adjective *greener* modifies grass and is linked by is; the adjective *well-kept* modifies yard and is not a predicate adjective, literally, **The greener grass is in the well-kept yard.**

Nouns as adjectives

We've already seen that some nouns such as *proper nouns* and *numbers* function as adjectives. There are lots more. In fact, it's one of the ways in which we've made communication more precise; almost every article in common use is modified in some way by a noun.

bags — We have garbage bags, grocery bags, litter bags, paper bags, trash bags and doggy bags (which our doggy never sees).

disks — There are compact disks, computer disks, disk brakes, disk harrows and spinal disks (though it's usually spelled *discs*).

houses — We describe them as brick houses, clapboard houses, tree houses, chicken houses, dog houses, etc.

rings — We want a diamond ring, a gold ring, a brass ring or even a key ring, but not a bathtub ring.

shelf — The pantry shelf, the closet shelf and the book shelf are part of the house; the rock shelf and water shelf are left outside.

shoes — We have leather shoes, canvas shoes, deck shoes, golf shoes and tennis shoes. (It's tiring just to think about it.)

tape — We use plastic tape, paper tape and computer tape as well as magnetic tape which we use on a tape recorder or tape deck.

In many cases the modifying noun has been joined to the noun it modified to form a new noun.

bookcase	book-end	bookplate	bookrack
bookshop	bottleneck	cameraman	carsick
cheesecake	cheesecloth	coattail	hatband
hatbox	hat-tree	lamplight	lamppost
landscape	piecework	seashore	shoehorn
shoetree	snakebite	snakeskin	snowball
snowcap	suitcase	teakettle	teammate
teamwork	teapot	teaspoon	textbook

The only way to tell if you have a noun-turned-adjective modifying a noun or a single noun made from two nouns is to consult a dictionary.

No one knows exactly how or why these changes come about, mostly because they don't happen all at once. A particular style may be used by a writer, then by another, until finally it gets picked up in a textbook or dictionary. There is often no universal agreement: one dictionary may list both styles, while another lists only one and ignores or condemns the alternative.

To recognize how haphazard the business is, you only need to browse through a dictionary. Why is *teacup* one word and *coffee cup* is two? Why are *teapot*, *teakettle* and *teaspoon* one word, but *tea bag* and *tea caddy* are two? And if a *teaspoon* is used to measure and stir tea, what in the world would you use a *tablespoon* for?

Textbook and *schoolbook* are the only books named by a single word. All others are just *books* whose function needs to be further clarified, as an *address book*, a *phone book*, etc. We expect a *textbook* to be a *schoolbook*, a book of instruction, but most books contain text unless they are *blank books*. Also, a *book jacket* is as much a part of a book as the *bookplate* or *bookbinding*, so why is *book jacket* two words? We refer to a *bookstore* or *bookshop* as a special place, but a *grocery store* or *clothing store* or *auto shop* is a generic place until it gets a modifier to describe its function.

A person who does *piecework* works with *piece goods*. A *lamp shade* sits on the *lamppost* from which you get *lamplight*. If a *bookkeeper* does *bookwork*, shouldn't a *beekeeper* do *beework*? Often the compound word doesn't even relate to what it describes. *Pocketbook* does not seem an appropriate name for a purse which is not a book and isn't likely to fit in a pocket.

Gender orientation and other offensive adjectives

Time for a brief political message. Just as there are offensive nouns, there are adjectives which can make someone's blood boil. *Cute* is not offensive unless you describe a grown woman as a *cute girl*. Not so long ago, *handsome* was used to describe only women, then only men; now we use it regardless of sex. Describing a young man as a *good boy* may be a compliment, but an Afro-American adult won't be so delighted. (Don't confuse *good boy* with that champion of southern compliments, *good old boy*.) The more aware you are of what you are saying, the more you will change and improve not only your speech patterns, but your vocabulary as well.

Many find the very term *politically correct* offensive, and well they might. We can get so careful not to offend, that our message is lost. Don't let that happen, but then, don't be thoughtless either.

Adjectives and vocabulary

Earlier we mentioned all of those words that we recognize, but don't use. Adjectives are where we find the most room for improvement and where we find the most new words. English contains a number of adjectives which can be adapted to most situations. Those are the ones we get in the habit of using and working to death; words like *adorable, crazy, fine, lovely, swell, terrible.*

As we recognize the overworked words and replace them, communication not only becomes easier, but it acquires new vitality and depth.

Adverbs

Adverb means *to a verb*, indicating that it is a word added to a verb, presumably to modify its meaning. Adverbs serve to clarify our message by qualifying an action or description as it relates to time, place, manner or degree.

Function

The function of an adverb is to modify a verb, an adjective or another adverb.

Adjective or adverb?

Adverbs are most commonly formed by adding *-ly* to an adjective, though not all adverbs end in *-ly* nor are all words which end in *-ly* adverbs. There are a considerable number of adverbs which take the same form as an adjective.

Fundamentally, an adjective modifies a noun whereas an adverb modifies a verb or adjective (which is, in turn, modifying a noun). Considering that each may perform, to some degree, the function of the other, that is, an adjective may modify another adjective and an adverb may modify a noun or pronoun, one may wonder why we require two separate parts of speech. Why don't we have a single part of speech called a *modifier* which combines the qualities of the adjective and the adverb? Beats me.

It is only fair to point out that there is no general agreement that an adjective may modify another adjective or that an adverb may modify a noun. Some find it easier to ignore exceptions to the rules, to claim that they are not accepted practice or to perform some other linguistic sleight-of-hand which accounts for their presence.

This section is primarily for those who recognize that the suggestion of a universal *modifier* is heresy and have a need to know more about adverbs. Everyone else should be content to use modifiers without distinguishing between the parts of speech, consulting a dictionary whenever necessary to confirm proper usage.

Basic Grammar — Putting It All Together

As for distinguishing an adverb from an adjective, you can usually tell by the way the adverb is used. Does it modify a verb, an adjective or another verb? Does it answer the question where, when, how, or to what degree?

Forms of the adverb

Adding *-ly* to an adjective is the most common form of the adverb; however, the adverb created in this fashion may have a meaning which differs from the root adjective.

Adjective —		Adverb —	
	bad		badly
	beautiful		beautifully
	calm		calmly
	charming		charmingly
	clever		cleverly
	cold		coldly
	famous		famously
	foolish		foolishly
	good		goodly
	hard		hardly
	large		largely
	late		lately
	near		nearly
	nice		nicely
	polite		politely
	several		severally
	severe		severely
	strict		strictly
	tender		tenderly
	willing		willingly

There are many adverbs which do not end in -*ly*.

again	here	how	now
quite	rather	seldom	since
soon	there	too	very
when	where	why	

Some adverbs are also employed as adjectives. This can be most confusing, for there are adjectives such as *hard* which double as adverbs and, additionally, form an adverb by adding -*ly*. *Dead* may be adverb or adjective, and the adverbial form deadly may likewise be adverb or adjective.

above	almost	courtly	daily
dead	deadly	easterly	far
fast	hard	hourly	late
least	less	little	lively
manly	much	near	oft
often	slow	southerly	stately
then	weekly	well	womanly

Nouns as adverbs

Nouns as adverbs only sounds confusing. It is simply a noun doing what the adverb usually does, modifying a verb. A noun used in this manner retains the property of a noun to take an adjective.

> **They are going** *camping*. *Camping* is a noun used as an adverb to tell *where they are going*.

> **They are leaving** *Monday*. *Monday* is a noun used as an adverb to tell *when they are leaving*.

> **They are leaving next** *Monday*. *Monday* retains the property of a noun which allows it to take an adjective; therefore, it has been modified by the adjective *next*.

> **We hiked seven** *days* **before turning back.** *Days* is an adverb/noun which takes the adjective *seven*.

Adverbs of time and place

An adverb clarifies the action of a verb or the description of an adjective by indicating proximity. It gives us a reference point in relation to the action or description.

> **They are leaving** *Monday* tells us *when* they are traveling.
>
> **They are traveling** *home* tells us *where* they are traveling to.

The adverbs *home* and *Monday* in the above sentences tell us something about the action: *when* they are going and *where* they are going. Adverbs may relate a wide range of information relating to time or place, some quite specific, some rather vague.

> **They are leaving** *now*.   **They are leaving** *eventually*.
>
> **They are leaving** *forever*.   **They are leaving** *here*.
>
> **They travel** *often*.   **They are traveling** *monthly*.
>
> **They are traveling** *backwards* around the world.

Adverbs of time and place answer questions like how soon? how often? before or after? for how long? where? in what direction?

Adverbs of manner and degree

Adverbs of manner and degree relate to the *properties* of the action or description; what is the *style* and how *complete* is the action or quality.

> **They left** *quickly*.   **They were dressed** *nicely*.
>
> **They departed** *willingly*.   **They treated us** *badly*.
>
> **They** *seldom* **spoke.**   **I** *rather* **like them.**   **I** *nearly* **fainted.**

Adverbs of manner and degree answer questions like how? in what way? to what extent?

Interrogative adverbs

Certain adverbs begin a sentence which asks a question.

When did you first realize that adverbs were out to get you?

Where do you think they came from?

Why don't you just burn this book?

How else do you plan to escape?

You can often identify an adverb as a word which *answers* a question beginning with *when, where* or *how?*

Comparisons

Adverbs may show comparison in the same fashion as adjectives, by adding *-er* to the adverb or preceding the adverb by *more* for the comparative, and by using *-est* or *most* for the superlative. There are, moreover, irregular comparisons similar to those of the adjective.

Base	Comparative	Superlative
badly	more badly	most badly
courtly	more courtly	most courtly
deadly	more deadly	most deadly
fast	faster	fastest
foolishly	more foolishly	most foolishly
hard	harder	hardest
little	less	least
much	more	most
near	nearer	nearest
often	more often	most often
tenderly	more tenderly	most tenderly
well	better	best
willingly	more willingly	most willingly

There are adverbs which cannot be compared because they represent an absolute or an unknown.

again	almost	before	ever
here	how	never	no
now	quite	since	then
there	too	very	when
where	why	yes	

Stuff to watch out for

There are more than a few adverbs maligned by the authorities at any given time. They should be forgiven (the authorities, that is; you can't forgive an adverb) because there is no way to reprint books as fast as the language changes. Today's improper use is often tomorrow's clever phrase. In spite of that self-inflicted warning, let's take a look at some.

Badly is a word that is often used badly, especially when we say that we feel badly about something. *Badly* is an adverb which means *improperly*, *imperfectly*, or *unpleasantly*.

> **She plays the guitar *badly*.**

> **He keeps our books *badly*.**

> **They managed their affairs *badly*.**

Substitute one of the synonyms for *badly* in these sentences and you will see that the word is used correctly. In short, you can *play, keep, manage, see, hear* or *run* badly, but you can't *feel* badly. Just drop in the synonyms and you will see that none fit. You might feel *imperfect* or *unpleasant*, but not *imperfectly* or *unpleasantly*. You may, however, feel *bad*.

The reason *badly* doesn't work is because you can't place an adverb after a linking verb. Remember, the linking verb has no other function except to link; therefore, you are attempting to modify the subject noun with an adverb and that is against the rules. The easiest way to be sure you are correct is to remember one of the synonyms for *badly* and try to substitute it. Or you might just try to learn some new synonyms for *bad* like *ill, sick, vile* or *evil*.

91

Good also seems to be a habitual offender. The reason is simple. Good is an adjective only and we often try to use it as an adverb in place of well.

She plays the guitar well.

He keeps our books well.

They manage their affairs well.

Nobody, no time, no how does nothin' *good*, but we can do anything *well.*

Real has a habit of dropping in to replace *really* at times. *Real* is an adjective that means *genuine. Really* is an adverb that means *actually* or is **used without precise meaning for emphasis. Really?**

She plays the guitar really well.

He keeps our books really well.

They manage their affairs really well. Really!

Almost turns into *most* when we get lazy. We know that *most* means the *greatest amount* and *almost* means *nearly*: nearly the best, nearly the worst, nearly *anything*. We get careless about pronouncing the *al-* and before long most becomes the word of choice.

She plays the guitar almost as well as her teacher. She knows most of the classics.

Won't belabor this with any more examples. You get the idea.

Prepositions

A preposition is one of those connectors that help tie thoughts together. The preposition itself is a word which indicates a relationship, generally one of position. The preposition and its object (normally a noun or pronoun) along with any modifiers of the object form the prepositional phrase. The prepositional phrase is a modifier, functioning in the manner of an adjective or an adverb, or the preposition with its object may be the subject of a sentence.

Function of the preposition

The function of a preposition is to show the relationship between words or groups of words in a sentence.

Commonly used prepositions

about	above	across	after
against	along	among	around
at	before	behind	below
beneath	beside	between	beyond
but	by	concerning	considering
down	during	except	excepting
for	from	in	inside
into	like	near	of
off	on	out	outside
over	past	pending	per
regarding	save	saving	since
through	till	to	toward
under	until	unto	up
upon	with	within	without

In addition, there are a number of phrases which function as compound prepositions.

according to	along with	as to
because of	by means of	by reason of
by way of	contrary to	for the sake of
in addition to	in accordance with	
in case of	in care of	in front of
in lieu of	in regard to	in reference to
in spite of	instead of	on account of
out of	with reference to	with regard to

Prepositional phrases

The prepositional phrase is the key to understanding prepositions. As described above, the prepositional phrase is comprised of the preposition and its object with any modifiers of the object.

above **the mahogany desk** — *Desk* is the object of the preposition *above*; *the* and *mahogany* are adjectives which modify *desk*.

behind **the old barn** — *Barn* is the object of the preposition *behind*; *the* and *old* are adjectives which modify *barn*.

during **her speech** — *Speech* is the object of the preposition *during*; *her* is a pronoun/adjective which modifies *speech*.

except **Sunday** — *Sunday* is the object of the preposition *except*.

outside **these walls** — *Walls* is the object of the preposition *outside*; *these* is a pronoun/adjective which modifies *walls*.

because of **you** — *You* is the object of the preposition *because of*.

contrary to **popular opinion** — *Opinion* is the object of the preposition *contrary to*; *popular* is an adjective which modifies *opinion*.

with reference to **your last order** — *Order* is the object of the preposition *with reference to*; *your* and *last* are adjectives which modify *order*.

Prepositional phrases in sentences

Used in a sentence, the prepositional phrase acts as an adverb or an adjective. The phrase itself is a relational modifier in that it describes something in relation to the noun, verb, adjective or adverb which it modifies.

> **The picture is** *hanging* **above the mahogany desk.** — *Above the mahogany desk* is the prepositional phrase modifying the adjective *hanging*. (Functioning as an adverb, it answers the question, *where?*) If the sentence were changed to **The picture above the mahogany desk is mine**, the prepositional phrase would be acting as an adverb, modifying the verb *is*.

> **The children** *are playing* **behind the old barn.** — *Behind the old barn* is the prepositional phrase modifying the verb *are playing*.

> **Dinner** *was served* **during her speech.** — *During her speech* is the prepositional phrase modifying the verb *was served*.

> **We open** *every* **day except Sunday.** — *Except Sunday* is the prepositional phrase modifying the adjective *every*.

> **Outside the wall** *is* **not safe.** — *Outside the wall* is a prepositional phrase used as a noun, the subject of the verb *is*. Think of it this way — *outside the wall* names a place and that place cannot be named except by the entire phrase.

> **Because of you, I** *will try* **again.** — *Because of you* is the prepositional phrase modifying the verb *will try*.

Words to watch

Inasmuch as the preposition describes a relationship, choosing the correct words for the prepositional phrase can be important to assure that you are conveying the correct message. Following is a sampling of the more common errors; some can convey a misleading message others are simply preferred form about which you have to make your own decisions.

> **About, around** — Preferred usage dictates that only *about* can be used to mean *approximately*. **We expect to arrive home in** *about* **three hours.**
> *Around* implies *encircling* or *circuitous*; however, some modern dictionaries do recognize *around* to mean *approximately* as a colloquialism and list *about* as a synonym. Take your pick.

Agree — *Agree to* is to give consent. **I** *agree to* **your plan.**
  Agree with is to be of one mind, to concur. **I** *agree with* **you about the plan.**
  We *agree to* a proposal and *agree with* a person.
  Dictionaries don't cut any slack on this one. See **concur**, below.

Among, between — Preferred usage dictates that *between* be used when two are involved, *among* when there are more than two.
  The two children split the candy *between* **them.**
  The marbles were divided *among* **five players.**
  Between, however, is often used for more than two. **It is a trade agreement** *between* **three nations.**

Behind, in back of — One of the definitions for *behind* is *at the back*, but if you want to indicate that one thing is *behind* another thing, use *behind*, not *in back of*, *in the back of* or *at the back of*.

Belong — *Belong to* is to be a part of a particular thing or group.
  We *belong to* **the club.**
  Castor and Pollux are two stars which *belong to* **the constellation Gemini.**
  Belong with should be used to describe things merely placed together.
  We *belong with* **the members of the club.**
  Castor and Pollux *belong with* **the stars in Gemini.**
  This distinction between *to* and *with* holds true for other prepositions as well which serve to express similar but slightly different meanings. (See **for, of, to and with**, below)

Beside, besides — *Beside* means at the side of or in proximity to; *besides* means in addition to or other than.
  The large picture sat *beside* **the small one.** The pictures are side by side or at least, near each other.
  There is another picture *besides* **the two on the mantle.** There is a third picture in addition to the two on the mantle.

Capacity — *Capacity of* calls for a specific quantity. **The tank has a** *capacity of* **twenty gallons.**
  Capacity for indicates indeterminate potential. **He has a** *capacity for* **understanding.**
  Capacity to indicates finite potential. **She has the** *capacity to* **win the race.**

Concur — *Concur in* indicates general agreement of the subjects. **We** *concur in* **our assessment of your plan.**

Concur on indicates agreement of the subjects in certain specifics. **We concur on several points (but disagree on others).**
Concur with is agreement between the subject(s) and another person. **I (we) concur with you on the merits of the plan.**
See **agree**, above.

Differ — To *differ from* is to be unlike. **The winters in New York differ from those in Florida.**
To *differ over* or *differ about* is to quarrel. **They differ over (about) the merits of the plan.**
To *differ with* is to merely disagree. **I must differ with your analysis of the findings.**

Different — It has oft been said that *different from* is the only correct form and that *different than* is incorrect. The British use it, why can't we?

Except — When you want to exclude something or someone, use *except*. **Take all of the furniture *except* the couch. Everyone passed the course except Charles.**
Traditionalists frown on the use of *outside of* for *except*, though modern dictionaries often acknowledge its use.
Accept means *to take when offered;* the use of *accept* or *accepting* is definitely wrong.

In, into — Which word you use depends on where you are. **They are running in the yard** tells us that they are running within the confines of the yard. **They are running into the yard** tells us that they are entering the yard from outside.

Inside, inside of, within — *Inside* refers to interior and should not be used to reference *time* or *distance*. Use *within* or *less than* to indicate approximations of time or distance. **We will be there *within* two hours. We ran out of gas *less than* five miles from home.**

More than, over — *More than* should be used to express quantity. **There are *more than* twenty students in the class.** Strictly speaking, *over* refers to relative position. Unstrictly speaking — ho hum.

Outside — Regardless of how you feel about using *outside of* to mean *except* (see **except**, above), you should not be comfortable using the phrase *outside of* when *outside* alone will do the job or especially when *outside* alone is more precise.
Outside the house alludes to all space that is not inside the

house, whereas **outside of the house** suggests the outer walls of the house.

Regard, regards — *Regards* is the plural form of *regard*. It is incorrect in the phrase *in regard to* or *with regard to*. To test it, substitute *relation* for *regard* in the phrases; then try *relations*.

Wait on — *Wait on* is often used incorrectly in place of *wait for*, which can be misleading. Wait on is to serve and wait for is to remain in readiness. **I will wait on my friends** implies that I will serve food, drinks, etc. **I will wait for my friends** indicates that I plan to be here when they are ready.

With — *With* usually means to be in the company of but may also denote opposition. It is well to be alert to statements which might have a dual meaning so as to clarify them. **Tom fought *with* John in court.** Did they oppose each other or together face a common adversary?

Things up with which I will not put

Prepositions perform a distinct function in the sentence. They should be used with forethought to help convey a message, not gratuitously to add clutter. In order to develop concise speech and writing patterns, avoid the use of prepositions which are unnecessary and add nothing to the clarity of the message.

Finally, there is that old business of ending a sentence with a preposition. In some situations it sounds awkward and should be avoided. In others, it's more awkward to avoid ending the sentence with the offending preposition. In most cases, the sentence can be reconstructed. Let's consider Mr. Churchill's statement.

This is the sort of English I will not put up with. Ends with a preposition; grammarians say it's wrong.

This is the sort of English up with which I will not put. Grammatically correct, but awkward; Mr. C. got a lot of laughs with this and so have many comedians.

I will not put up with this sort of English. All of the fun is taken out, but it does convey the message.

Conjunctions

Conjunction is the state of being joined together. Grammatically, a *conjunction* is the word or group of words which forges the link. Simple conjunctions which are most familiar are *if, and , or* and *but.* In addition to joining, the conjunction implies a relationship between the things joined and that is the characteristic which makes the choice of conjunction so very important. A poor choice can change the message which you are attempting to convey.

Function

The function of a conjunction is to form a bridge between two or more words or groups of words.

Coordinate and subordinate

The two main classes of conjunction are identified not by the conjunctions themselves, but by their function.

The **coordinate conjunction** is typified by the joining of two or more elements of equal standing within the sentence. The elements joined may be single words or groups of words.

> apples *and* oranges   running *and* jumping
>
> blue *or* green   large *or* small   to *and* fro
>
> the yellow airplane *and* the small car
>
> the dogs of war, *and* the cat's meow
>
> Peter, Paul *and* Mary played *and* sang at the concert.
>
> Jack declined to go *because* his car was out of gas.
>
> I like your idea, *but* we must act immediately.

However diverse these elements might seem, they have equal standing in that one is not dependent on the other within the context of the sentence. Note that the phrases in the compound sentences could stand alone as separate sentences indicating that they are not dependent on each other.

The **subordinate conjunction** is one that joins a subordinate clause to an independent clause. The subordinate clause is often a modifier and the subordinate conjunction may begin the sentence or join elements within it.

When my ship comes in, I'll be at the train station.

History judges a politician not by the candidate's promises, *but* by the incumbent's deeds.

Except for all the pain, exercise is fun!

She reveled in her victory, *although* her opponent was stung by the defeat.

This diet lets you eat all you want, *only* don't swallow.

Apply the same test here as for the *coordinate conjunction* and you will see that you can divide the sentence into one phrase which can stand alone as a sentence and one which can not.

List of conjunctions

Most of the words in the following list have come up in discussion of other parts of speech. They are often used as conjunctions while maintaining the characteristics of another part of speech.

after	also	although	and
as	because	before	both
but	either	except	for
however	if	lest	neither
nevertheless	nor	notwithstanding	
only	or	provided	save
seeing	since	so	still
than	that	then	therefore
though	unless	until	what
when	where	whereas	whereat
whereby	wherefore	wherein	whereof
whereupon	wherever	whether	while
without	yet		

If you have a need to know how a word is being used in a specific instance, your only recourse is to carefully study the sentence and break it down. If you reach the wrong conclusion, take heart in knowing that practice will improve your performance and that in most instances two grammarians would likely disagree as well.

Correlative conjunctions

Remember the old admonition about *neither, nor?* that you must use *neither* with *nor* and *either* with *or?* Well, that is still true, and there are other conjunctions which are used in pairs as well. The admonition about using them together is not so stern, for many of the examples cited here do just as well with a different partner or even standing alone; however, both members of the team are often required for clarity.

as, as — I feel *as* confident about this *as* you do.

as, so — *As* the parent goes, *so* goes the child.

both, and — I am *both* surprised *and* pleased at the outcome

either, or — *Either* Judy *or* I will see that the food is ready.

if, then — *If* it rains, *then* we'll cancel the picnic.

neither, nor — *Neither* Judy *nor* I care to participate in the ceremony.

not only, but also — *Not only* is the food attractive, *but also* tasty.

now, then — *Now* we'll plan the trip, *then* we'll figure out how to pay for it.

though, yet — *Though* we live apart, *yet* we'll still be friends.

whether, or — *Whether* we like the idea *or* not, we have to go through with it.

Other connectives

There are other connectives which are not conjunctions, but which exhibit some conjunctive force in linking independent clauses or the dependent clause of which they are a part to an independent clause. These words are variously described as *coordinate* or *subordinate, independent or dependent, conjunctive adverbs or relative adverbs, linking* or *transitional*. For now, we'll view them as conjunctives for which we have no particular set of rules. Look them over and note any that are familiar, add a few of your own and we'll deal with their proper use in the section on **sentence structure.**

accordingly	afterwards	again
as a result	at last	at the same time
as well as	besides	consequently
conversely	doubtless	eventually
evidently	finally	for example
for instance	for this reason	further
furthermore	hence	how
in addition	in any case	indeed
in fact	in like manner	in short
likewise	meanwhile	moreover
namely	nevertheless	next
nonetheless	now	on the contrary
on the other hand	otherwise	perhaps
possibly	that is	thus
whenever	whereby	wherein
why	wherefore	

Interjections

Interjections lost much of their impact with the demise of the melodrama. Picture fair young maid, head thrown back, wrist touching forehead, uttering deathless lines like *Oh, woe is me!* , *Alas!*, and *Horrors!* Then the inevitable closing line as the moustached villain dressed in morning coat and top hat slinks out muttering *Curses! Foiled again!* Oh, well.

Probably the best reason for reading this section is to find something socially acceptable to say when hammer strikes finger.

The interjection changes the pace of the narrative and (hopefully) catches the readers attention.

Function

The function of an interjection is to express a sudden emotion or reaction.

Commonly used interjections

An interjection can be almost anything you choose. Words that emulate sounds, like **Biff! Bam! Boom!** Adjectives that are usually modifiers can be transformed to show high emotion, like **Beautiful! Excellent!**

ah!	alas!	congratulations!
good grief!	great!	help!
hey!	hooray!	hurry!
my goodness!	never!	no!
no way!	oh!	ouch!
outstanding!	ugh!	what!?
wow!		

Punctuation

Normally a strong interjection is punctuated by an exclamation point (!), or perhaps two or three. An exclamation that is part question might be punctuated by both an exclamation point and a question mark (!?). A mild exclamation may take only a comma. More in the section on **punctuation!**

Now that you know all about the parts of speech and how to use them correctly, put what you know into practice.

Begin by paying attention as you read through this book. You'll find lots of things you don't agree with. Newspapers are a great source of grammatical errors, because so much copy is written under such tight time constraints that the editors can be relied on to miss a lot!

Rest assured that once you develop the habit of paying attention and looking critically at what you read, it will become automatic and, at the same time, your vocabulary will miraculously begin to improve.

SENTENCE STRUCTURE

Wouldn't want to insult your intelligence by reminding you that a sentence is a group of words expressing a complete thought or that it begins with a capital letter and ends with a period, question mark or exclamation point. You'll just have to remember that from English 101. And if you've been reading e e cummings, you won't believe me anyway.

There is no embarrassment in telling you that effective communication depends on your ability to construct a sentence well. Simple sentences are just that — simple. As long as you pick the right words, there's not much chance of going wrong. Expressing more complex thoughts, however, requires a bit of organizational skill. You need to be sure that a sentence is laid out in such a way that it transmits exactly the message you intended. Only a word separates from pointing out a fat cow to the boss's wife to calling the boss's wife a fat cow.

Phrases and clauses

So far we've discussed the words that make up the language. Now let's put some of those words together.

A *phrase* **is comprised of two or more related words which do not express a complete thought.** You might think of it as a snatch of consciousness: a brief glimpse of reality such as a description of something, a bit of action or a place.

The phrase can be a **noun phrase** which is a noun or pronoun and its modifiers,

a man   the woman   a small child

the slim runner   a funny clown   busy baker

a black and white dog   a singing bird   a big bug

the tall tree   the fragrant red rose   a deserted street

a dimly lit Italian restaurant   antique furniture

Noun phrases (continued)

> sparkling water   carpenter's tools   smelly trash
>
> crisp clean air   bright gold   cracked old teapot
>
> the long black sleek shiny chauffeured limousine

a **verb phrase**, which is a verb with its modifiers,

> are digging furiously   were dancing gracefully
>
> smiled politely   spoke loudly
>
> hurriedly entered   aimed carelessly
>
> was eating sparingly   is nervously tapping

a **participial phrase**, a participle with its modifiers and complements,

> slowly driving the car   turning the page
>
> spoken with pride   walking the dog
>
> called on the phone   trembling with anticipation
>
> taking the time   swelling with pride

a **prepositional phrase**, which is a preposition with its object and modifiers,

> toward the white house   up the stairs
>
> in the back yard   concerning the latest proposal
>
> like the blue sea   over the garden wall
>
> under the bridge   during the night

or an **infinitive phrase**, an infinitive with its complements and modifiers.

> to make a touchdown   to work in the garden
>
> to begin the beguine   to touch your toes
>
> to drive the red car   to build a bookshelf
>
> to help a friend study   to sing like an angel

A *clause* is a group of related words which includes the thing talked about (noun, pronoun, or noun substitute) and the action or condition attributed to that thing (verb). A clause may be *independent* or *dependent*.

An **independent clause** expresses a complete thought which can stand alone as a sentence.

A **dependent clause**, also called a **subordinate clause** does not express a complete thought and therefore can not be a sentence by itself. It must be supported by an independent clause.

Think of an *independent* clause as the base of a sentence which expresses a complete thought. The *dependent* or *subordinate* clause serves to modify some portion of that expression and is *dependent on* or *subordinate to* the independent clause.

In the following examples, the dependent clause is underlined.

> The board is in agreement <u>regarding the selection of a chairman.</u>
>
> You should run for exercise <u>while you watch your diet.</u>
>
> It sounds like a great band <u>even if it is too loud.</u>
>
> She called yesterday <u>to ask you to drive to the store</u>.
>
> Someone will be held responsible <u>for the mistakes that were made</u>.
>
> <u>Everywhere she went</u>, she spoke with pride.
>
> This violin, <u>which she has been playing for years,</u> is her most treasured possession.

Note that in the next to the last sentence, the dependent clause begins the sentence and in the last sentence, it is in the middle. There are no restrictions on placement of the dependent clause other than that its meaning should be clear. A cleverly turned phrase will pique a reader or listener's interest, but nothing is gained if the meaning is lost.

Essential parts – subject and predicate

The essential parts of a sentence are the subject and the predicate. The listener needs to know *what is the thing we are talking about* and *what do we have to say about that thing?*

The subject, the thing we are talking about

The subject may be the name of a single thing, or it may include the names of several. It may be simply the name, or it may include an elaborate description. Whatever its characteristics, however many or few words comprise it, the entire subject is called the **complete subject**. Following the section above on **phrases** there is a list of noun phrases, any of which qualifies as a complete subject.

The **simple subject** is the noun or pronoun by itself, without any modifiers. It is the simple subject to which the verb, or predicate, refers and which determines the form of the verb (see the section on **Relationships**).

Throughout the earlier sections on **nouns** and **pronouns**, there are numerous examples of both. Taken alone, without modifiers, any one of those nouns or pronouns is a *simple subject*.

The **compound subject** is made up of two or more nouns or noun clauses.

> *Bob* and *Jill. . .*   *The children* and *the adults. . .*
>
> *The fragrant red rose* and *the big black bug. . .*
>
> *Hunting* and *fishing. . .*   *What you see* and *what you get. . .*

Elements of the subject

The subject of a sentence is usually one or more nouns or pronouns modified by adjectives and adverbs which comprise the *noun phrase.* The subject may take other forms, however, such as a noun clause, a prepositional phrase, a gerund phrase or an infinitive phrase.

108

A **noun clause** is a dependent clause which takes the place of a noun and can be the subject of a sentence.

> *What you see* and *what you get* are two different things. A compound subject made up of two noun clauses. If the sentence were revised to *What you see* is *what you get* we have a subject *What you see* which is a noun clause and an object of the verb which is also a noun clause.

A **prepositional phrase** often indicates a place in relation to its object so that the subject is not the object itself, but the *somewhere else* described by the prepositional phrase. Clear?

> *Under the car* is a pool of water. *Under the car* defines the subject place which neither *under* nor *car* can describe by itself.

A **gerund phrase** is a verbal posing as a noun (you may recall) with its modifiers.

> *Living well* is the best revenge. *Living well* is a concept which is the subject for the verb *is.*

An **infinitive phrase** is made up of a verb, usually preceded by *to,* and its modifiers. The infinitive may function as a noun or a verb and can take an adverbial modifier.

> *To understand completely* is most difficult. *To understand* is the subject of the verb *is*; *completely* is an adverb which modifies understand.

The predicate, what we have to say about the subject

The predicate describes the action or condition attributed to the subject. The predicate may make one or a number of assertions about the subject. Like the subject, the attribute may be a single word (a verb) or an elaborate description (a verb with modifiers). The entire predicate, whether a single word or several, is the **complete predicate.** Following the section above on **phrases** there is a list of verb phrases, any of which qualifies as a complete predicate.

The **simple predicate** is the active or linking verb alone, without modifiers. It is the word which describes the action of the subject or links the subject to the expression which describes the condition of the subject.

Within the section on **verbs**, above, there are listed a number of action and linking verbs, any of which qualifies as a simple predicate.

The **compound predicate** is comprised of two or more verbs (simple predicates) joined by a conjunction.

> smile and sing   run and jump
>
> beg, steal or borrow   aimed and fired
>
> <u>ran</u> part of the time <u>and</u> <u>walked</u> part of the time

Elements of the predicate

The predicate of a sentence is comprised of a verb which may take adverbial modifiers as well as direct and indirect objects with their adjectival and adverbial modifiers. (Try to say that five times fast.)

An **action verb** alone is the very minimum form of the predicate.

> She *ran.*   He *swam.*   They *drove.*

A **linking verb**, which does not express action, must have a noun, pronoun or adjective to complete its meaning.

In the following examples, the verb complements are underlined.

> The weather here *is* <u>very damp</u>.[*linking verb — is*]
>
> The spring flowers *have* <u>a fragrant aroma</u>.[*linking verb — have*]
>
> This *must have been* <u>a beautiful place</u>.[*linking verb — must have been*]
>
> Our visit *has been* <u>most pleasant</u>.[*linking verb — has been*]

The **direct object** names the recipient of the action.

In the following examples, the direct object is underlined.

> **The lead guitar just *lost* two <u>strings</u>.** [*verb — lost*]
>
> **We *sent* him a <u>message</u>.** [*verb — sent*]
>
> **She *read* the <u>book</u>.** [*verb — read*]

The **indirect object** describes to or for whom the action was taken.

In the following examples, the indirect object is underlined.

> **We *sent* <u>him</u> a message.** [*verb — sent*]
>
> **They *ate* <u>lobster</u> for lunch.** [*verb — ate*]

Sentence types

Here's another item that's tough to work into casual conversation, but, hey, you just might want to know about it — There are four basic styles of sentence depending on the manner in which a thought is expressed.

The **declarative sentence** makes a direct statement.

> **I just made a new batch of root beer.**

The **interrogative sentence** asks a question.

> **Would you like some?**

The **imperative sentence** gives a command or makes a request.

> **Help me carry the keg to the basement.**

The **exclamatory sentence** expresses sudden emotion.

> **Hey! Don't hog it all!**

Simple sentence

All of the examples given on the last two pages are simple sentences. A simple sentence is merely a single independent clause with no dependent clauses. Simple doesn't necessarily mean short, any more than compound or complex means long. A simple sentence can contain a number of phrases or very long phrases which make it seem complicated at first glance. The following example illustrates the point.

> **The lumber, paneling, siding, roofing shingles and hardware were loaded on the truck and taken to the building site.** Six items (a compound subject) were *loaded and taken* (a compound predicate) equals one simple sentence.

Compound sentence

The compound sentence is made up of two or more independent clauses (or simple sentences) which have been combined into a single sentence. The compound sentence does not contain any subordinate clauses.

> **It's summertime. The living is easy. The fish are swimming. The cotton is high.**
> **It's summertime, the living is easy, the fish are swimming and the cotton is high.**

> **I thought thanksgiving was over. There are turkeys all around me.**
> **I thought thanksgiving was over, and there are turkeys all around me.**

Complex sentence

The complex sentence is a simple sentence with one or more dependent clauses.

In the follow examples, dependent clauses are underlined.

> That was a beautiful beach <u>we passed on the road</u>.

> <u>When you arrive</u>, please call me.

> The girl <u>who won the pie eating contest</u> is my sister.

> <u>Before you go</u>, kiss the cat good-bye.

Compound-complex sentence

A compound-complex sentence is a compound sentence which also has one or more dependent clauses.

In the following examples, the dependent clauses are underlined.

> I thought thanksgiving was over, and the turkeys <u>who rule the world</u> are all around me.

> <u>Whenever it is convenient</u>, you wash the car and I'll mow the lawn.

Compound-compound-complex sentence

Just kidding!

Incomplete sentence

Can we discuss this? Do you want to? Lets!

We speak in fragments. In words carefully molded to create a timeless impression like *okay!* *oh, yeah?* *forget it!* *why not?* *says you!* *cream and sugar,* *here!* *on the desk.*

But we don't write like that. Do we? Should we?

Communication is not merely words. If it were, everything written and spoken would be presented in a formal style according to a set of exacting rules. Instead, we change the order of our words and chop up our sentences in an endeavor to communicate our feelings and emotions, and to excite those same feelings in our listener. We want to impart a little of ourselves in our communication, which we often do when speaking. Writing is another matter. We have a chance to look things over, to decide whether or not they sound right, and to make changes. The results are frequently stiff and formal when that is not the impression we mean to convey. Whenever practicable, therefore, we should write the way we speak in order to give our writing a more personal touch and to keep it interesting.

Writing in the manner we speak requires that we regularly overlook or at least stretch the conventional rules. This section on **sentence structure** begins, *Wouldn't want to insult your intelligence. . . .*It could have said, *I wouldn't* or the editorial, *We wouldn't* or that great unknown entity, *Nobody would.* Whatever it *could* have been, the subject is superfluous to the point of the sentence. Some might concede that the subject is understood, while others would discard it as *not a sentence* and take off two points.

The reason for all of this preamble is not to advocate incomplete sentences, but to acknowledge that we may legitimately write sentences which seem incomplete from someone else's point of view, and we must always be alert to the danger of incomplete, *meaningless* or *misleading* sentences.

Whenever you attempt to communicate in a cryptic style, you run the risk of assuming too much. If a colleague enters your office with a cup of coffee in one hand and a sheaf of papers in the other while you are busy on the phone you might fire off a quick, "On the desk!" and turn away. What you don't realize until you turn quickly and spill it, is that the coffee, not the pile of papers, was left for you.

> **The door slammed and the calculator fell off the desk. He yelped in pain as it hit his foot.**

Not the error of incomplete sentences, but certainly one of assuming too much. What hit his foot, the door or the calculator? (Or is the reader being presumptuous by assuming that this is not explained earlier or later in the narrative?)

Let's take a look at a brief business communication:

> **Dear Ms. Rogers,**
>
> **I received a message that you called on the 25th at 4:30 PM.**
>
> **Your order for 25 widgets shipped today, the 26th.**
>
> **I do hope that this meets with your approval.**
>
> **I am sending this with my kindest personal regards.**
>
> **S. Kinsky**

Supposing, instead, that Mr. Kinsky dashed off a really brief note.

> **Ms. Rogers—**
>
> **Got your message. Order shipped. Hope you approve.**
>
> **Regards, S. Kinsky**

This sort of abbreviated informal communication is not uncommon, so it seems perfectly acceptable even though there is not a sentence in sight. However, Mr. Kinsky is not aware that there was another phone message and a letter, each containing different instructions and neither of which he received. Nor is he aware that his undated fax message didn't get through until the next day.

Let's try again.

> **Ms, Rogers—**
>
> **Received your phone message of the 25th at 4.30.**
>
> **Shipped your order for 25 widgets on the 26th.**
>
> **Hoping you approve.**
>
> **Best regards,**
>
> **S. Kinsky**

If you are uncomfortable writing incomplete sentences, by all means, avoid them. On the other hand, a so-called incomplete sentence often conveys a message which is more personal or dramatic. Just be sure it conveys the correct message, and don't overdo it.

RELATIONSHIPS

Relationships in grammar refer to the consistency of word forms used in a phrase, a clause and a sentence. Few things in a narrative stand out so much as a lack of agreement between the elements of a sentence.

Agreement of subject and verb

The verb should always agree with its subject in person and number. This means that if the subject is in the first person, the verb must be in the first person and if the subject is singular the verb must be singular.

Following is the conjugation of the verb **to be**, the most used and unfortunately, the most irregular of verbs; however, there is a pattern to its forms which makes them relatively easy to remember.

	Singular	Plural
Present tense		
First person —speaker	I **am**	We **are**
Second person —spoken to	You **are**	You **are**
Third person —spoken of	He, she, it **is**	They **are**
Past tense		
First person —speaker	I **was**	We **were**
Second person —spoken to	You **were**	You **were**
Third person —spoken of	He, she, it **was**	They **were**
Future tense		
First person —speaker	I **shall be**	We **shall be**
Second person —spoken to	You **will be**	You **will be**
Third person —spoken of	He, she, it **will be**	They **will be**

Note that *are* is the plural form for all three persons in the present tense and that *were* is the plural form for all three persons in the past tense; that *be* is the plural for all three persons in the future tense with the helper *shall* in the first person and *will* in the second and third. Note also that the singular forms are the same as the plurals with just four exceptions: *am* is the first person present singular, *is* is the third person present singular and *was* in the first and third person past singular.

Following is the conjugation of the verb **call** which is also set up to make its pattern easily discernible.

	Singular	Plural
Present tense		
First person —speaker	I **call**	We **call**
Second person —spoken to	You **call**	You **call**
Third person —spoken of	He, she, it **calls**	They **call**
Past tense		
First person —speaker	I **called**	We **called**
Second person —spoken to	You **called**	You **called**
Third person —spoken of	He, she, it **called**	They **called**
Future tense		
First person —speaker	I **shall call**	We **shall call**
Second person —spoken to	You **will call**	You **will call**
Third person —spoken of	He, she, it **will call**	They **will call**

Call is a regular verb and, as you can see, the conjugation is much simpler than it is for *to be*. All forms in the present tense are the same except for the third person singular. The past tense is one form, as is the future tense with the addition of the modifiers, *shall* and *will*.

Refer to the section on **verbs** for a more complete conjugation of the verbs *to be* and *call,* the rule for forming the past tense of regular verbs and a list of the principal parts of the most common irregular verbs.

It seems simple enough to follow the conjugation tables above, but more complicated expressions require some special considerations, particularly when the correct form doesn't sound right.

Verb with a compound subject

Usually the compound subject joins two or more elements and is therefore plural.

> **John and Robert *are* driving to Mexico.**

When two or more elements are described as alternatives, that is, one or the other, the subject is singular.

> **Neither John nor Robert *is* driving.**
>
> **Either John or Robert *is* driving.**

Sometimes two elements which are joined refer to the same person or thing and are singular.

> **The wife and mother *is* also a distinguished lawyer.**

Sometimes the elements joined form a unit and are a *dilemma*.

> **Meat and potatoes *is* the customary evening meal.**
>
> **Meat and potatoes *are* the customary evening meal.**
>
> **Potatoes and meat *is* the customary evening meal.**

If you consider *meat and potatoes* as a single entity, the first sentence is correct. There is a school of thought, however, which says that when there are two or more items in the subject which disagree in number, the verb should agree with the nearest subject as in the second and third sentences above. It's up to you; pick the rule you like or the sentence which you think sounds best.

A word of caution — Make sure that it is clear to your audience whether you are referring to one person or two.

> **The president and chief operating officer *attends* all of the board meetings.** Singular verb — implies that a single person fills both positions.
>
> **The president and chief operating officer *attend* all of the board meetings.** Plural verb — presumes that we are talking about two different people or the writer selected the wrong verb form.
>
> **The president and chief operating officer both *attend* all of the board meetings.** Meaning is clarified by the use of *both*.

Elements modified by a limiting adjective such as *each* or *every* are singular.

Each car and each truck *is* licensed separately.

Every doctor and every lawyer *is* not a crook.

An adverb such as *also, often, perhaps* or *usually* which precedes one of two singular elements joined by *and* modifies the verb in relation to that one element. The verb is therefore single, inasmuch as it relates to each element separately.

The car, and also the truck, *is* to be washed.

One egg, and often a spoonful of grits, *is* served for breakfast.

The politician, and perhaps his aide, *is* telling the truth.

John, and usually his wife, *attends* the conventions.

Naturally, if each element is plural the verb is plural.

Eggs, and often grits, *are* served for breakfast.

Modifying phrases

Modifying phrases which intervene between the subject and the verb never change the relationship between the two. Such phrases should be ignored when attempting to determine that the subject and verb are in agreement. Intervening phrases in the following sentences are shown in italics.

John and Robert, *after a quick trip home to pack,* are driving to Mexico.

The wife and mother, *holder of several degrees,* is also a distinguished lawyer.

Meat and potatoes, *plain but nourishing,* is the customary evening meal.

Each car and each truck, *regardless of the number of owners,* is licensed separately.

Every doctor and every lawyer, *regardless of what people say,* is not a crook.

119

When a plural isn't a plural

Up until now we've assumed that we can easily identify a noun as singular or plural with the possible exception of *meat and potatoes*. There are (naturally) other, similar combinations like *ham and eggs* or *nut and bolt*, which need to be considered in the context of the sentence.

A nut and bolt *is* required for assembly.

A nut and bolt *is*(?) on the workbench.

A nut and (a) bolt *are* on the workbench.

There are nouns like *scissors*, *trousers* and *pliers* which are plural and take a plural verb. Nobody knows why. However, if you say a *pair of scissors* or a *pair of trousers* or a *pair of pliers* which sounds like *more* than one they become singular. Nobody knows why that is, either.

The trousers *are* on the floor.

The pair of trousers *is* on the floor.

There are other nouns which are plural in form, but singular in meaning, such as news, politics, economics and mathematics.

The news *is* all good.

Politics *is* the name of the game.

Economics *is* far from an exact science.

Mathematics *is* the science of numbers.

Proper names of individuals and companies are usually singular even though they take a plural form.

Mr. Brothers *is* an excellent physician.

Chrysler Motors *is* fighting hard to compete.

Collective nouns take a singular verb when considering the noun as a cohesive group and a plural verb when considering its diversity. (See **Collective nouns**.)

Weights and measures and other stuff

Nouns which express quantity, weight or volume may be singular or plural depending on the context.

Five dollars *is* all I have left. Singular —*five dollars* is one unit.

Five dollar bills *are* all I have. Plural —*bill* is a unit; *five . . . bills* is more than one or plural.

Ten pounds *is* enough to fill the bag. Singular — *ten pounds* is a unit.

Half of the land *has* been ravaged. Singular —*the land* is a unit.

Half of the workers *have* left. Plural — *half of the workers* implies more than one person. (What do you say if you started with only two workers? Beats me!)

Some of the sandwiches *are* left. Plural — *some of the sandwiches* implies more than one sandwich.

Most of the punch *is* gone. Singular —*the punch* is a unit.

Pronoun with antecedent

Remember antecedents? That's the noun which is later represented by a pronoun. **The pronoun must agree with its antecedent in gender, person and number.**

Gender agreement

Gender agreement is uncomplicated in most situations.

Bob showed us *his* new car. Janet showed us *her* new car.

Janet and Bob showed us *their* new car.

Note that the plural makes no distinction by gender. If, however, the pronoun refers to only one of the nouns connected by *and*, the pronoun takes the gender of its antecedent.

Janet and Bob showed us *her* father's new car.

In the case of a limiting conjunction, such as *or* or *nor*, there are choices: offer both options, let the pronoun agree with the nearest antecedent, eliminate the pronoun or change the noun form.

> **No man or woman has ever given so freely of *his or her* time.**
>
> **No man or woman has ever given so freely of *her* time.**
>
> **No woman or man has ever given so freely of *his* time.**
>
> **No man or woman has ever given so freely of time.**
>
> **None have ever given so freely of their time.**

The first three statements are decidedly awkward. The simplest solution to this problem, and most like it, is reconstruction. The fifth sentence will usually make the point. If it is necessary to mention *man or woman* elimination of the pronoun as in the fourth sentence loses nothing. Incidentally, if the object of the verb were tangible, such as a car, the indefinite article could be comfortably substituted for the pronoun.

> **No man or woman has ever given a car.**

Agreement of person

Our motto is *Don't change persons in mid-stream.* A sentence should not start out in one person and end in another.

> **If anyone wants to join me, *you're* welcome to come along,** doesn't cut it. **If anyone wants to join me, *he's* welcome to come along,** is correct, but it runs into that old gender problem. Why not just say, **Anyone who wants to join me is welcome to come along**?

When a pronoun follows two or more connected nouns and is referring to only one of them or neither of them, be sure that it is understood what the pronoun is referring to.

> **Neither Janet nor Joan are living in *her* new apartment.** Say, what? Whose new apartment? Perhaps *her* relates to an earlier reference and if it doesn't, this sentence should be reconsidered.

PUNCTUATION

Punctuation is how you tell the reader when to take a breath.

Not far from the truth. Correct punctuation helps your reader comprehend your message. It also gives you some control of the pace of the narrative to further convey your feelings. And it you didn't tell some readers when to breath, they just might explode.

Uses of the period

The period is used to end a sentence, to end an abbreviation and to punctuate the elements in an outline.

End of a sentence

The period is used to indicate the end of a sentence not otherwise ended by a question mark, exclamation point or the period following an abbreviation.

It is also be used to indicate the end of an incomplete thought injected into a narrative.

> **As the car turned the corner, she let out a scream.** *A high pitched, piercing shriek.* **Then she fainted.**

Abbreviations

The period is used to indicate an abbreviation, although it is optional for some. See **Abbreviations**, in the reference section.

Outlines

In outlines, the period is used optionaJlly after letters or numbers designating sections and sub-sections.

The question mark

The question mark is used to indicate an interrogative and to mark textual data as questionable.

To mark the end of an interrogative

The question mark is used to mark the end of any sentence that asks a question (no kidding?), including a question in a quotation,

"Is it time to leave?" she asked.

or a declarative sentence formed as a question.

It's time to leave?

In imperative sentence which makes a request will take either a question mark or a period.

Will you please leave?

Will you please leave.

See also **Exclamation point**, below.

Within a sentence

The question mark is used optionally within a sentence to add emphasis to a multiple query.

**Do you want to do this in three easy lessons, one hard one or not
at all?**

**Do you want to do this in three easy lessons? one hard one? or
not at all?**

The question mark may be used in parenthesis within a sentence to show that there is some question about the information which precedes it.

I expect to arrive at noon (?) on Tuesday.

The exclamation point

The exclamation point is used to mark the end of an exclamatory sentence.

Watch out for that tree! (George! George! George of the jungle.)

Will you please leave!

The exclamation point is used after an interjection or after any word used as an interjection.

Hey!   **Excellent!**   **Help!**   **Beautiful!**

The exclamation point adds emphasis to imply a sense of urgency and to capture the reader's attention.

Look! Good grief! Get out of here!

The interrobang

The interrobang is a combination of question mark and exclamation point to emphasize those statements which engender both wonderment and a strong emotional response: not quite a question, but certainly questionable.

She did what?!

A recent study financed by the government reached the conclusion that people don't like to go to the dentist because they fear pain?!

[Author's note: The interrobang was created by the author of a book by the same name. My copy was passed along and efforts to locate another have been to no avail. Any information about the book or the author would be appreciated and can be sent to the publisher of this book. JR.]

The uses of the comma

The comma is used to separate elements within a sentence, follow the opening of an informal letter, follow the closing of any letter, separate the elements in a date, separate the elements in an address, separate a persons name from his or her title and to section off large numbers.

Separating elements within a sentence

Here's one you are going to have to think about. Like mother said, it's for your own good. There are a number of rules which recount in great detail precisely how and when to use a comma. Most of them can be condensed into three simple rules.

> **Rule #1: Use a comma *only when it is necessary* to assure that the message will not be misunderstood.**

> **Rule #2: Don't use a comma if it is *not necessary* and especially if it might obscure the meaning of a sentence.**

> **Rule #3: Never forget Rule #2.**

The comma should be used to **set off any phrase or clause which might otherwise be misread**. Here's the part where you have to concentrate. Avoid the temptation to drop in a bunch of commas just to break up a long sentence. Take a look at the sentence and try to recognize how it might be misread. Look for words and phrases which are incidental to the flow of the main body of the sentence and need to be set off by commas. Look at long sentences which have independent clauses which need separation. Find the natural breaks in the flow of a sentence; the places where a reader might pause to grasp a concept before moving on. Following are some tips to help you along.

Separate dependent clauses and phrases which are incidental to the main body of the sentence.

> **It's difficult to discuss politics, *even local politics,* without getting emotional.**

> **After the party, *an elegant affair,* they went to the theater.**

Separate independent clauses in a compound sentence, particularly if they are long and divergent.

> **The meeting lasted most of the afternoon, and they had to face the long drive home.**
>
> **He learned his craft in the small theaters scattered throughout the country, but now he was playing Broadway.**

Use a comma to separate a word which interrupts the flow of a sentence such as a mild interjection or a connective which modifies a clause even if it is at the beginning of a sentence. See **conjunctions** for a list of the modifiers.

> **The team fought hard to keep up the pace and, *consequently*, they won.**
>
> ***Furthermore*, the movie was lousy.**
>
> **I can't believe you mean that, *Susan*.**

Do not interrupt the flow of a thought or split a clause by placing a comma between the subject and its verb or between the verb and its object. **The team fought hard, to keep up the pace and . . .** Wrong!

Do not use a comma to replace a conjunction. **The team fought hard to keep up the pace, consequently they won.** Wrong!

Do use a comma to follow the connective when a semicolon is used as the conjunction.

> **The team fought hard to keep up the pace; consequently, they won.**

Do use your own good judgment! Read the sentence over after it has been punctuated. Don't hesitate to take out any commas that interrupt the flow unnecessarily and don't hesitate to add a comma if the sentence sounds like a runaway freight train.

Elements in a series

For the sake of clarity, words and clauses in a series need to be separated.

> **The dress comes in four colors: aqua, pink, orange or black.**
>
> **He set out to streamline the office, trim the budget, and increase the output.**
>
> **She competes in the 50 yard dash, hurdles and cross country run.**

The final comma before the conjunction is optional. Use if you need to for clarity or just because you like it. Other than for clarity, whichever form you adopt should be consistent throughout your document.

Independent modifiers

Independent modifiers are those modifiers which are not dependent on or directly associated with any other modifiers; two or more which modify the same member should be separated by a comma.

> **The *long, black* station wagon drove down the *dusty, winding, dirt* road.**

Quotations

Use a comma to separate a direct quotation from its source unless it is superseded by other punctuation.

> **She said, "I want to see the play."**
>
> **"I want to see the play," she said.**
>
> **"May I go to the play?" she asked.** Comma superseded by the question mark.

Opening and closing of a letter

Traditionally, the opening of an informal letter is followed by a comma,

Dear John,   Dear Susan,

and the closing of any letter is followed by a comma.

Very truly yours,   Sincerely yours,

Dates and addresses

The parts of dates and addresses are separated by commas.

January 27, 1993	**27 January, 1993**
Memorial Day, 1992	**the fourteenth of April, 1992**
2030 Belle Vue Way, #81	**118 East 28th Street, Suite #408**
Tallahassee, FL 32304	**New York, NY 10016**

Grammatical conventions aside, the Postal Service has instituted an incentive program for business which precludes all punctuation on address labels. Undoubtedly, financial considerations will dominate, so that before long it may be commonplace to eliminate punctuation from all addresses which doesn't seem to be in any way detrimental to aesthetics or function.

Names and titles

Titles after a name are normally separated by a comma, as are the elements of a name when they are reversed.

John M. Chavin, M.D.	**James Mahoney, Esq.**
Chavin, John M.	**Mahoney, James**

Numbers

Commas are used to separate the thousands in large numbers.

81,548	**7,071,639**	**346,931**

The colon

The colon is used at the end of a clause to indicate that a word, a list, a phrase or another clause is to follow. It is used after the opening of a business letter and it is used after a division of time or literary reference to indicate that a subdivision follows.

The colon is used to end a clause introducing a list of items.

> **The parts of speech are as follows: Nouns, Pronouns, Verbs, Adjectives, Adverbs, Prepositions, Conjunctions and Interjections.**

The colon is also used to highlight a clause to follow.

> **As you go through life, remember one thing: The most humiliating criticism is indifference.**

Traditionally, the colon has followed the salutation in the opening of a business letter.

> **Dear Sir: To whom it may concern: Dear Madam:**
>
> **Dear Sir or Madam, as the case may be:** (My personal favorite)

Although some companies cling to this form, most prefer the personalized greeting followed by a comma. Now used primarily for occupant mailings, the demise of this very impersonal form has been hastened by the personalized computer letter.

The colon is used after a division of time, literature, etc. to indicate that a subdivision follows.

> **3:45 P.M.**   **15:45:17**
>
> **Isaiah 65:17**   **Psalms 23:1**

Semicolon

The semicolon is used in place of a conjunction or in place of a comma.

In place of a conjunction

The semicolon is used to join two independent clauses with or without a modifying connective.

> **Sharon has a managerial position; she enjoys the rights and privileges which go with the responsibility.**

> **Sharon has a managerial position; therefore, she enjoys the rights and privileges which go with the responsibility.**

In place of a comma

There are situations which call for a comma where the use of a semicolon is preferred in the interest of clarity. Think of it as two-tier punctuation with the semicolon as the stronger element of the two.

A sentence containing a combination of incidental words, lists of words, clauses, or phrases which requires a comma before a conjunction might be clearer if a semicolon were used before the conjunction.

> **We carefully planned the trip, packed the car and were ready to set out for the campground; but our plans went awry when the car, an old Buick with failing brakes, refused to start.** A comma could be used before *but*; however, the semicolon is a stronger indicator in contrast to the commas, and further serves notice to your reader to take a well-earned breath. If the sentence were **We carefully planned the trip, packed the car and were ready to set out for the campground, but our plans went awry** and ended there, the comma is not a bad choice.

A list of phrases or clauses is best separated by semicolons, particularly if the clauses are punctuated by commas.

> **Among the things we packed for the trip was the small, green tent; two sleeping bags; a selection of fresh and freeze-dried foods; the lantern, with fuel for two nights; an assortment of pots, pans and eating utensils; and a change of clothes.**

As with the comma, don't overuse the semicolon and don't hesitate to use it when it clarifies your meaning.

The apostrophe

The apostrophe is used to show possession, to show plurals for symbols and to indicate missing letters in a contraction.

Showing possession

The apostrophe is used with *s* to show the possessive form of nouns which do not end in *s*.

> **one man's hat**   **many men's hats**   **that woman's hat**
>
> **two women's hats** **this lawyer's case**
>
> **the day's end**   **the dog's bone**   **this theory's premise**

The apostrophe is used alone to show the possessive form of nouns which end in *s*.

> **the pliers' jaws**   **the scissors' edge**   **Mr. Jones' car**
>
> **two authors' books**   **those hens' eggs**

Singular nouns ending in *s*, such as *Jones* may also take an apostrophe *s* ending: it's the writer's choice.

132

The possessive of more than one taken together as a unit is shown by making the last member possessive.

> **Joan and Bob's house is on the outskirts of the city.**
>
> **The restaurant and bar's Oriental decor is striking.**

To indicate individual ownership, make each member possessive.

> **Joan's and Bob's houses are outside the city.**

Plurals for symbols

The plural for individual letters, numbers and signs are indicated by apostrophe *s*.

> **Mind your p's and q's.**
>
> **They are at 6's and 7's.**
>
> **Can we use #'s to indicate pounds?**

Contractions

The apostrophe is used to indicate the position of missing elements in contractions.

> **don't**   **aren't**   **won't**   **haven't**
>
> **the summer of '42**   **in November '86**

About quotation marks

Quotation marks are used to set off direct quotations; titles of articles, poems, works of art and such; and special words or phrases such as slang, technical terms and nicknames.

Direct quotations

Only the exact words of the speaker or writer are enclosed in quotation marks.

> **She said, "I want to go, but only if we leave by dawn."**
>
> **"There is nothing to fear, but fear itself."**

Quotation marks are omitted for any quotation or portion thereof which is quoted indirectly.

> **She said that she wants to go, but "only if we leave by dawn."**
>
> **She said that she wants to go, but only if we leave by dawn.**

Either of the above two examples is correct, but only the second part of the sentence may be enclosed in quotation marks because they quote the speaker's exact words.

Punctuation within quotations

A *period* or a *comma* is always placed before the closing quotation mark.

> **John said, "The report is due this week."**
>
> **"The report is due this week," said John.**

The speaker is always separated from the quotation by a comma whether at the beginning of the sentence as in the first example above, or ringed by the quote as in the following example.

> **"The report is due next week," said Joan, "and it must be delivered on time."**

Note that the quotation starts with a capital letter, but the second part of a split quotation does not, unless it is a new sentence.

> **"The report is due next week," said Joan. "It must be delivered on time."**

134

The *question mark* or *exclamation point* is enclosed within the quotation marks when it applies only to the quote and outside the quotation marks when it applies to the entire sentence. Punctuation is not required within the quotation marks when punctuation is placed after the closing quotation mark.

> **"When do you need to leave?" he asked.**
>
> **Who said, "I think, therefore I am"?**

Any other punctuation in the sentence remains the same as it would be without a direct quotation.

Titles

Titles of short works such as magazine articles, essays, songs, poems, paintings and sculpture are set off by quotation marks. The rule of thumb is that anything long enough to appear in book form including plays, opera, collections of art, etc. are underlined or printed in italics. All other titles are set off by quotation marks.

Extraneous material in quotes

Quotation marks are used to direct attention to special words in a sentence such as slang, technical terms, colloquialisms, nicknames and material referred to elsewhere in the sentence.

Note that such highlighting may also be achieved by underlining, or printing in italics or bold face.

Single quotation marks

Single quotation marks are used in the same manner as double quotes to set off material already contained in double quotes — in effect, to set off a quotation within a quotation.

> **"I think she said, 'be ready by noon,'" Tom reported.**

The hyphen

The hyphen is used to join the parts of certain compound words.

mother-in-law   **pre-Columbian**   **weak-headed**

It may also be used to create an expression comprised of several words which are to be taken as a unit.

cock-of-the-walk   **holier-than-thou**

A hyphen is placed after the syllable of a word divided at the end of a line to indicate that the balance of the word follows on the next line.

The dash

A dash indicates a break in the flow of a sentence, usually to insert a parenthetical remark or for emphasis.

> When I passed the house — the one at the end of the block — it was empty.

> There's only one thing that can save us — Superchicken.

Parentheses and brackets

Parentheses are used to separate incidental information which would otherwise interrupt the flow of the sentence.

> We set out on July 27 (Susan's birthday) to tour the area.

Parentheses are often used to separate confirming numbers in a sentence.

> The admission price is eight dollars ($8.00) for advance reservations and ten dollars ($10.00) the day of the show.

Parentheses set off letters or numbers which are used in a sentence to enumerate items in a list.

> **Our goal is to see that you (a) understand the proper use of English and (b) use your knowledge to communicate effectively in the language.**

Parenthesis may be used to indicate lower level subdivisions in an outline. For example, the first, second, third, etc. levels might be, in order, I (Roman numerals), A, 1, a, (1), (a).

Incidentally, *parentheses* is plural; one (parenthes?) is a *parenthesis*.

Brackets are used to insert editorial commentary; that is, to indicate that the material inserted is not a part of the original material.

> **He said that they [the Jones family] have only lived in this area for six months.**

> **The letter mentioned, "there [sic] inability to cope."** The word *sic*, Latin for *thus*, is used in this context to show that the preceding word or phrase has been quoted verbatim and in the opinion of the one making the insertion is incorrect or at least questionable.

Indicating omissions - the ellipsis

The ellipsis (*plural* ellipses) is a series of three dots (or periods) used to indicate the omission of a word or words. When used at the end of a sentence, it is followed by the ending punctuation.

> **She said, "The report . . . is unacceptable."** The missing material is descriptive information which is not germane to the writer's point: that the report is unacceptable.

To improve readability - leaders

A line of periods, called leaders, is used to track the eye across the page of an index, a tabulated page or such.

Units sold this year 10,462
Defective units returned 9,248

CAPITALIZATION

The rules for capitalization are relatively clear and easy to follow; however, the writer often has options because there is no way to spell out every contingency, and even if it were possible, someone would disagree.

Words and phrases

The basic rule for capitalization specifies that proper nouns and adjectives are to be capitalized and that common nouns and adjectives are not capitalized. There are, however, many proper nouns which have become common, common nouns used with or as proper nouns, and titles of respect which are capitalized common nouns. Let's try to sort it out.

Names of individuals

The name of a person, whether real or fictional, is always capitalized.

John Jones   **Suzy Smith**   **Mark Twain**
Samuel Clemens   **Alfred E. Neumann**

Titles

Titles or degrees which precede or follow a name are always capitalized.

Mr. John Jones   Rev. Suzy Smith   Hon. Mark Twain

Samuel Clemens, Esq.   Alfred E. Neumann, Ph.D.

Ordinarily, a title such as reverend, president or doctor is capitalized only when used in conjunction with a proper name; however, titles of position or respect may be capitalized at the writer's discretion when the title clearly refers to a particular person.

Our President will be out of the office all week.

We're playing golf with the Doctor in the morning.

Organizations

The proper name of an organization is always capitalized.

Chamber of Commerce   Mothers Against Drunk Driving

Florida State University   Justice Department

Bank of America   Ford Motor Company

A department within an organization is capitalized at the writer's discretion (or the company's edict).

Art Department or art department

Sales Department or sales department

Shipping Department or shipping department

Products

Names of products which are trade names are capitalized.

Coca Cola   Cadillac Seville   Mountain Dew

Many trade names such as Kleenex and Vaseline are commonly used generically; technically, however, they refer only to the product of the company which owns the rights to the name and should be capitalized.

Works of art

The words in the title of a work of art: painting, sculpture, music, play, etc. are capitalized except for articles, prepositions and conjunctions unless they are the first word in the title. *The* used before the title is not capitalized unless it is at the beginning of a sentence or part of the title.

> **Whistler's Mother**   **the Mona Lisa**
>
> **The Glorious Victory of the Sloop Santa Maria**
>
> **Death of a Salesman**   **Swan Lake**

Publications and documents

The words in the title of a publication, an article, an essay, or a document are capitalized except for articles, prepositions and conjunctions unless they are the first word in the title. *The* used before the title is not capitalized unless it is at the beginning of a sentence or part of the title.

> **War and Peace**   **Poor Richard's Almanac**
>
> **The Sea and the Jungle**
>
> **Zen Flesh, Zen Bones**
>
> **the Declaration of Independence**
>
> **My Life and Hard Times**

Academics

School subjects are not capitalized unless they are a word which would be capitalized under another rule or are the name of a specific course.

> economics   **Economics 101**
>
> French   **Intermediate French**
>
> programming   **Programming in COBOL**
>
> computers   **Computer Basics**

Place names

The name of a building, monument, place or region is capitalized. The directions north, east, south and west are not usually capitalized, but may be when used to reference a specific region. *The* used before a name is not capitalized unless it is at the beginning of a sentence or part of the name.

Empire State Building	Hancock Building
Sears Tower	Eiffel Tower
Vietnam War Memorial	Great Wall of China
Jefferson Memorial	Washington Monument
Tiger Balm Gardens	the Gaza Strip
Times Square	Little Italy
Monroe Township	the Hoosier State
the Wild West	the Eastern Seaboard
the Orient	the East (referring to the Orient)
Rocky Mountains	England and France
French Riviera	Grand Canyon
the South Pole	the Battery (an area in New York City)

Events and Holidays

Special events, historic periods and holidays are capitalized.

the Winter Olympics	the World Series
Bach Festival	Senior Prom
Nicene Council	War of 1812
Elizabethan Age	Roaring Twenties
Christmas Day	New Year's Eve
Labor Day	Thanksgiving

Religious references

Most religious references are capitalized including names of religions, denominations, religious groups, deities and sacred works.

Christian	Judaic	Islam
Hindu	Buddhist	Shinto
Presbyterian	Mormon	Methodist
Lutheran	Seventh Day Adventist	
Holy Trinity Church	Southern Baptist Convention	
Temple Beth-El	Missouri Synod	God
Jehovah	Jesus	Yahweh
Holy Ghost	Allah	Shiva
Almighty	Astarte	Zarathustra
Holy Bible	Koran	the Vedas
Apostles Creed	Sermon on the Mount	

Names of rites and services are generally not capitalized.

worship service	baptism	seder
matins	confession	bar mitzvah

Pronouns referring to deities are capitalized at the writer's discretion.

In His service   **Jesus and his ministry**

Scientific and technical terms

The rules for terms of a scientific or technical nature are the same as for other terms: capitalize only proper nouns or adjectives. Doubtless many of the terms are unfamiliar, and the only recourse is a good dictionary.

142

Relationships

References to a relative are not capitalized unless they are used with a person's name or used in place of the person's name.

Cousin Edith   Uncle John

Let me help you, Mother.

My sister is visiting this week.

Calendar

The names of the days and months are capitalized; whereas the seasons of the year are not unless they are personified.

Monday   Tuesday   Wednesday

January   February   March

winter   spring   summer   fall

Where is Winter, with his icy chill?

Compound and hyphenated names

Compound names which include a proper noun or adjective require that the proper name be capitalized, but not the common noun.

Darjeeling tea   Irish linen

Italian spaghetti   French pastry

Swiss chocolate   Turkish bath

Cincinnati chili   New Orleans jazz

Florida oranges   Asian flu

Hyphenated names are capitalized.

Schleswig-Holstein   Jacques-Louis David

Proper nouns and adjectives with prefixes are capitalized, but the prefixes are not capitalized.

pro-American   anti-French

pre-Cambrian   ex-President

Capitalization in a sentence

The first word in a sentence is always capitalized, whether a complete sentence, a fragment or an interjection.

The pronoun *I* is always capitalized.

The first word in a direct quotation is capitalized if the quotation is itself a complete sentence.

> He asked, "If you're so busy, how come you have so much time to tell me about it?"

When a complete sentence follows a colon, the first word of that sentence should be capitalized.

> Please remember this: Fear of failure is worse than failure.

Capitalizing to show respect or for emphasis

Usually, reference to high office is capitalized to show respect.

the Queen   the President   the Pope

As indicated above, we may capitalize lesser titles when they clearly refer to a particular individual. We may also want to capitalize to show respect or emphasize the involvement of an unnamed individual, group or thing.

> **The Accountants reported that we are not over budget.**

> **The Engineers report that we are on schedule.**

> **There is nothing wrong with the Printing Press; it is the Paper that created the problem.**

Just don't overdo it or the emphasis value will be lost.

NUMBERS

There is an abundance of rules for dealing with numbers in text and, as with most things, there is no universal agreement. The most important criterion is to protect the readability of your document and to be consistent.

Figures or spelled out

There is a guideline which says that a number should be spelled out if it is less than ten or divisible by ten.

one	two	three	four	five
six	seven	eight	nine	ten
twenty	thirty	forty	fifty	sixty, etc.

According to this rule, *one million, nine hundred forty-seven thousand, six hundred and eighty* should be written out, but it's doubtful that the creator of the rule had that in mind.

Another rule suggests that it is acceptable to write out any number of up to two words, which sounds reasonable.

All rules recommend consistency; that is, all of the numbers in a sentence *in series or related* should be either written as figures or spelled out. That is the best piece of advice contained in any rule.

Rules aside, common sense should prevail. The way in which numbers are expressed will depend largely on how many numbers there are, how large the numbers are and the type of document in which they are appearing.

Round numbers

Numbers which are approximations are usually written out to avoid confusing them with exact numbers.

> **There are about three thousand rules of grammar, but most people can agree on just two. Unfortunately they can't agree on which two.**

Approximations which would be too wordy if written out may be expressed in newspaper headline style; i.e., a number followed by the word *million, billion*, etc.

> **The population of New York City is approximately 7.1 million.**

Numbers in combination

Often a sentence will contain more than one number or set of numbers which relate to different items. Each number, or set of numbers should be assessed individually as to how they will be presented with consistency, not only in the one sentence, but in any related sentences in the narrative.

> **We have six runners for the 100-yard dash.**

> **Our inventory includes ten 25-watt bulbs, eight 50-watt bulbs and fourteen 100-watt bulbs.**

Numbers beginning a sentence

If it is at all avoidable, don't begin a sentence with a number. If, however, it is necessary, spell out the number at the start of the sentence regardless of how the rest of the numbers in that sentence are presented.

A FEW SPELLING RULES

Reading this section will not make you an expert speller. It will, however, help you to become a better speller. Modern English, including scientific and technical terms, comprises well over a million words. We may have a nodding acquaintance with as many as 50,000 of those words, but we use, on a regular basis, a few thousand at most and are plagued by the spelling of a few hundred. Learning about the construction of words alerts you to patterns which tell when spelling is most likely right, and allows concentration on those most likely wrong. Don't be put off by the meager examples in each section. They are there only to illustrate the point; be assured that there are always more words which follow a rule than there are exceptions.

As much as I hate to admit it, your old English teacher was right: If you don't know how to spell a word, look it up. Naturally, if you don't know the first letter of the word, you may have to look in more than one place. Sure, it's a pain, but if you are really interested in using the right word, consider one other thing your teacher probably forgot to tell you. Looking up the word can often prevent a misunderstanding. For example, it's good news if you *brake* your car, but not so good if you *break* it. Among those words often misspelled are a number of similar sounding words which mean quite different things such as *affect/effect, ascent/assent, adapt/adopt, altar/alter* and *accept/except.* See what I mean?

Dual spelling

Matters are further complicated by the words which have acceptable dual spellings. Common practice within our own sphere of influence (frequently requiring approval of instructor or supervisor) generally dictates which form we use. Many options such as *programme* are seldom used in America. The older forms of *-our* and *-re* as the last syllable of a word have generally been replace by *-or* and *-er* respectively. We tend to prefer *labor* to *labour, color* to *colour* and *center* to *centre,* but we use *theatre* as often as *theater.* Perhaps those in the theyatuh feel it smacks of culture. Common practice, however, does require consistency; whichever spelling you choose should be used all of the time.

acknowledgment acknowledgement

adviser advisor	analog analogue
caliber calibre	catalog catalogue
center centre	encase incase
enclose inclose	encyclopedia encyclopaedia
endorse indorse	enquire inquire
enrollment enrolment	fledgling fledgeling
gipsy gypsy	gray grey
judgment judgement	maneuver manoeuvre
medieval mediaeval	naturalise naturalize
orthopedic orthopaedic	practice practise
pretense pretence	reflection reflexion
smolder smoulder	theater theatre

Pronunciation

Looking up a word occasionally is the mark of a conscientious, careful writer; looking up the same word over and over again may imply something quite different. These few pages are a small effort to assist in the quest to be identified as something other than "quite different". Like most of us, you have millions of unused brain cells lying fallow; it is time to put them to work.

Careless pronunciation is a trap. Perhaps you want to describe something clever or inventive as *ingenious*, only you get careless and pick up *ingenuous*. *Ingenuous* means frank or sincere. Not bad, really, but not what you wanted to say.

Pronunciation is definitely an aid to proper spelling. It's usually much easier to spell a word correctly when you pronounce it properly, or to look it up when you are not quite sure.

Pronunciation can help in another way. When you look up a word, try pronouncing each syllable phonetically with a brief pause between syllables, taking care to pronounce each letter (even silent ones) and never varying the pronunciation of a particular letter. The result is a strange word which you wouldn't care to have another hear you say aloud, but one which will trigger your subconscious to tell you how to spell the word the next time you see it. Take *phonetically*, for example. Spelled the way it's normally pronounced, the results look like *fonetekly*, which could set the reader to looking for a German dictionary. Mentally sounded out one syllable at a time, however, it comes out *pho* (using a soft *f* or *p-ho* in our mental pronunciation to indicate *ph*), *net* (I can spell that), *i* (that, too), *cal* (and that), *ly* (and here's a bonus: pronouncing *cal* and *ly* separately insures that both *l*'s will get into the final spelling). You don't have to do this very many times before it becomes automatic and you stop looking up the same words over and over again.

The A-B-C's are not for children

Remember the cute rhyme in nursery school? See the colorful cards on the wall containing gaily decorated letters of the alphabet? You should have known what was to come when the colorful letters were replaced by stark black and white cards, capitals and lower case, with lines carefully drawn top, bottom and through the middle. You should have known that if you survived penmanship they would find another way to get you. And they are out there, singly and in groups.

We tend to concentrate on vowels because they give us the most problems. Just five vowels, *a, e, i, o, u* and one part-time vowel, *y*, are responsible for about twenty vowel sounds. Now any mathematician will tell you that it is no problem to create twenty distinct combinations out of five vowels. Unfortunately, this is English where any one of the sounds might come from several different spellings (*meat, meet, mete, deceit*) or any one spelling may engender a number of pronunciations (*rouge, rough, gouge, cough, thorough*).

Consonants are equally treacherous. The letter *s* masquerades part time as *z* (*suppose*), as *sh* (*sugar*), or quietly hides (*aisle, isle*). The *c* vacillates between being an *s* (*cede*) and a *k* (*care*) when it's not being an *sh* (*ocean*) or hiding behind a *k* (*acknowledge*). And the *k* - outrageous! Blatantly stands at the beginning of a word doing nothing (*knock, knee, know*). Almost as bad is the *p*, which normally well-behaved, when put with an *h*, thinks it's an *f* (*physician, phobia*). Association with *p* is not the only diversion of the *h*. Put it with a *g* and it can't decide whether to sound off like an *f* (*tough*) or be silent (*light*). Which brings us back to one of the same problems that exists with vowels, a single sound created by different spellings (*fool, photo, laugh*).

It's a wonder we can write this language at all. But these things have not been revealed to you to discourage you. By no means! They have been pointed out only to make you wary and to thirst for battle, so go forth and conquer - but be careful out there.

Tips about vowels

Unfortunately, there are no rules which can be applied consistently, however some of these may help when you think you know the spelling, but have a lingering doubt.

Silent -e

Many words having a long vowel sound in the last syllable take a silent -*e* at the end in contrast to similar words which have a short vowel sound.

bid	bide	bit	bite	cap	cape
hid	hide	hop	hope	kit	kite
mop	mope	rid	ride	slop	slope

Doubling vowels

Often the long *e* sound is achieved by doubling the vowel in contrast to the single *e* in a similar word.

bet	beet	fed	feed	met	meet
per	peer	wed	weed		
red	reed	—though we also have *read*, which may sound the same as either *red* or *reed*, depending on use			

Unfortunately, there are numerous exceptions, most of which add *a* to the spelling instead of a second *e*.

bed	bead	best	beast	men	mean
net	neat	pet	peat	set	seat

In the case of the letter *o*, doubling often creates a short *u* sound.

cop	coop	hop	hoop	hot	hoot
lop	loop	lot	loot	mod	mood
rot	root	tot	toot		

A short vowel sound, in contrast to a long vowel sound in a similar word, often signals the presence of a double consonant.

baring barring	biter bitter	caned canned
caper capper	coper copper	cuter cutter
hoping hopping	later latter	moping mopping
plater platter	taped tapped	

-ei- and -ie-

In at least one Chinese dialect the long sound of *i-e* properly inflected is a cry of distress. It is also appropriate for English spelling.

Let's begin with the rule you learned in school — "*i* before *e* except after *c*." That's easy enough . . . when it works. What your teacher forgot to tell you is that it works (almost always) *only* with the long *e* sound.

achieve	believe	ceiling	chief	conceit
conceive	deceive	grief	niece	perceive
piece	receive	relieve		

Words pronounced with a sound other than the long *e* don't follow the rule.

deign	feign	feint	freight	heifer
heir	height	neigh	neighbor	reign
reins	seismic	their	veil	vein
weigh	weight			

Some words with the long *e* sound are spelled contrary to the rule.

either	financier	leisure	neither	seize
specie	weird			

Prefixes

Normally a prefix added to a word changes its meaning without changing spelling. There are exceptions. (Who could have guessed?)

The good news is that the exceptions are modest and clear cut or of little concern to us here. Into the latter category fall words such as *inhabitable*, which means the same as *habitable*. The prefix *in-*, which means *not*, has been added without changing the spelling of the root word, but the meaning has not changed and both words are in common use. Compare that with *human* and *inhuman*. It's another "nobody knows why" situation.

The exceptions to the rule that spelling does not change all involve hyphens:

> Hyphenate when joining *ex-*, *all-* or *self-* to a noun, such as *ex-president*, *all-inclusive*, or *self-proclaimed*.

> Hyphenate when the prefix is used with a proper noun or adjective, such as *pro-American* or *un-American*.

> Hyphenate to alleviate confusion such as creating a word which could be confused with another (*re-creation*, the act of creating again versus *recreation*, amusement) or to make the word easier to recognize (*re-emerge* rather than *reemerge*). You have some latitude with this one, but as in all things, be consistent.

There are about fifty prefixes in general use and nothing is to be gained by listing them all; however, it will be helpful to know the meaning of some which are often confused:

> *ante-* means *before* as in *antedate*
> *anti-* means *against* as in *antibody*
>
> *dis-* means *separation* as in *disgrace*
> *dys-* means *ill* or *bad* as in *dysfunction*
>
> *hyper-* means *above* or *excessive* as in *hyperactive*
> *hypo-* means *under* or *beneath* as in *hypodermic*
>
> *per-* means *through* as in *pervade*
> *pre-* means *before* as in *precede*
> *pro-* means *forward* as in *proceed*

Suffixes

Dumping the silent -*e*

Usually, when a suffix beginning with a vowel (-*ed*, -*ing*) is added to a word with a final silent-*e*, the -*e* is dropped before the suffix is added.

bake	baked	baker	baking
brave	braved	braver	braving
home	homed	homer	homing
kite	kited	kiter	kiting
manage	managed	manager	managing
mope	moped	moper	moping
skate	skated	skater	skating

As you might expect, there are exceptions. After *c* or *g* the -*e* is retained before a suffix beginning with *a* or *o* (are you with me so far?) in order to preserve the soft sound of the *c* or *g*.

embrace embraceable	notice noticeable
outrage outrageous	trace traceable

Words with the suffix *-ment* keep the silent *-e* when it is preceded by a single consonant.

achieve achievement	**appease appeasement**
atone atonement	**induce inducement**
move movement	**place placement**

When the *-e* is preceded by two consonants it is usually dropped,

judge judgment   **acknowledge acknowledgment**

In England the *-e* is not dropped, and the form appears as an optional spelling in many American dictionaries. Just keep in mind that if you opt for the British spelling, do it that way all the time.

Finally, there are some common exceptions just to make sure that no one gets an A on the exam.

dye dyeing	**hoe hoeing**
involve involvement	**mile mileage**
singe singeing	**true truly**
whole wholly	

Doubling consonants

Following the silent *-e* rule, we drop the *-e* when adding endings like *-ed* and *-ing*. But how about their counterparts, the words with short vowel sounds which have no silent *-e*? How do we keep from confusing the two words? Simple. We double the consonant so that while *mope* becomes *moping*, *mop* becomes *mopping*. This usually works, but as you might have guessed, we don't get off that easily.

The above rule applies only to syllables that contain a single vowel so that *scoop* changes to *scooping* (**not** *scoopping*).

Basis Grammar - Putting It All Together

Words of more than one syllable require a further consideration, namely, which syllable is accented. Uh, oh!, we're back to pronunciation again. If the accent of *the word created* is on the last syllable before the suffix, follow the doubling consonant rule above.

confer con-fer´ring   defer de-fer´ring

deter de-ter´ring   refer re-fer´ring

If the accent of *the word created* is not on the last syllable, do *not* double the consonant.

confer con´fer-ence   credit cred´it-ing

defer def´fer-ence   refer ref´er-ence

-er versus *-or* ending

The *-er* ending indicates the person, thing or action related to the root word and is the more common ending. Whenever in doubt, *-er* is the ending to use.

blow blower	cook cooker	deal dealer
eat eater	govern governer	leap leaper
learn learner	pay payer	read reader
speak speaker	teach teacher	weep weeper

Some words take only the *-or* ending.

actor	creditor	elector
elevator	governor	visitor

And a few words take either ending.

adviser	advisor	embracer	embracor
operater	operator	vender	vendor

155

-cede, -ceed, -sede endings

Only one word uses the *-sede* ending — **supersede.**

Three words use the *-ceed* ending.

      exceed   **proceed**   **succeed**

All other words use the *-cede* ending.

      concede   **procede**   **recede**   **secede**

Memorize the four exceptions and you have one spelling lesson down pat!

Y as a vowel

We don't normally include *y* in our list of vowels, because it performs that function only part time. At the beginning of a word or syllable, it tends to function as a consonant; whereas, when it follows another consonant it functions as a vowel. If you wonder why anyone cares, read this sentence again, aloud, paying particular attention to the *y* sounds. In *you* and *paying,* it exhibits a hard sound, while in *why* and *anyone* it sounds like the *i* in *while.* Never mind that phonetic spelling could eliminate the *y,* we're concerned here with how to get along with it.

A final *y* preceded by a consonant changes to an *i* before all suffixes *except* those suffixes beginning with *i.*

fry	**fried**	**frying**
copy	**copier**	**copying**
rely	**relied**	**relying**
sixty	**sixtieth**	**sixtyish**
try	**tried**	**trying**

A final *y* preceded by a vowel generally doesn't change when a suffix is added,

boy	boyish	
play	played	playing
pray	prayed	praying
stay	stayed	staying
stray	strayed	straying

except sometimes. Go figure.

day daily	gay gaily	lay laid
pay paid	say said	

Hard c

As mentioned earlier the letter *c* often hides behind a *k*; this time you get to put it there. Words ending in a hard *c* add a *k* before suffixes beginning with the vowels *e* or *i*.

mimic	mimicked	mimicker	mimicking
panic	panicked	panicking	panicky
picnic	picnicked	picnicker	picnicking
traffic	trafficked	trafficker	trafficking

Suffixes beginning with *a* are added to the word ending with a hard *c* with no change in spelling.

angelic angelical	critic critical
mimic mimical	pragmatic pragmatical
specific specifically	systematic systematically
terrific terrifically	

Plurals

Forming a plural offers another challenge to the writer. Most plurals are formed by adding *s*.

author authors	baker bakers
butcher butchers	chief chiefs
clown clowns	doctor doctors
lawyer lawyers	manager managers
master masters	plumber plumbers
servant servants	teacher teachers

There are, however, enough exceptions to keep it interesting and to keep those who are concerned about being correct close to a dictionary.

Irregular nouns

The bad news is that one group of irregular nouns changes spelling in a random fashion.

addendum addenda	alumnus alumni
child children	crisis crises
criterion criteria	datum data
die dice	foot feet
goose geese	man men
medium media	mouse mice
ox oxen	tooth teeth
woman women	

Another group of nouns doesn't change at all.

deer	fish	hose	gross	moose
salmon	series	sheep	species	vermin

And yet another group allows you to make a choice.

appendix	appendixes	appendices
beau	beaux	beaus
brother	brothers	brethren
cactus	cactuses	cacti
criterion	criterion	criteria
focus	focuses	foci
formula	formulas	formulae
gymnasium	gymnasiums	gymnasia
hippopotamus	hippopotamuses	hippopotami
index	indexes	indices
medium	mediums	media
memorandum	memorandums	memoranda
radius	radiuses	radii

Must not forget those words which are always plural, even when referred to in the singular.

alms	clothes	forceps	gallows
nuptials	pants	pliers	remains
riches	scissors	shears	suds
tongs	trousers	victuals	

The good news is that most of these words are in common use and you will seldom encounter any which are unfamiliar.

Nouns ending in -f and -fe

Another erratic group are those nouns ending in -f and -fe. Some take an s to make the plural,

chef chefs **chief chiefs** **dwarf dwarfs**

159

whereas others change the *f* to *v* and add *s* or *es*,

calf calves	half halves	knife knives
shelf shelves	thief thieves	wife wives

and others leave it up to the writer to choose.

beef	beefs	beeves
hoof	hoofs	hooves
loaf	loafs	loaves
scarf	scarfs	scarves
wharf	wharfs	wharves

Nouns ending in *s*, *ss*, *z*, *sh*, *ch*, and *x*

Forming the "yet another group" group are nouns ending in *s*, *ss*, *z*, *sh*, *ch*, and *x*. If you can just remember that list of endings, you are home free - they (almost) all take *es*.

ax axes	bush bushes	couch couches
dress dresses	loss losses	marsh marshes
match matches	punch punches	push pushes
ranch ranches	tax taxes	waltz waltzes

And still there are exceptions: for example, the plural of **gross** is **gross**.

Nouns ending in -*y*

The letter *y* gets a little friendlier here. If a -*y* ending is preceded by a vowel simply add *s*.

boy boys	day days	display displays
play plays	quay quays	tray trays

If a -*y* ending is preceded by a consonant, change the *y* to *i* and add *es*.

beauty beauties	family families	lady ladies
memory memories	pansy pansies	theory theories

Compound nouns

These offer an interesting challenge. Really! Most compound nouns are made up of a subject and a modifier. In most cases, you have only to decide which is the subject or principal word and apply the rules for making it plural.

Easiest to deal with are the one word compounds.

bookcase bookcases	bottleneck bottlenecks
cameraman cameramen	cheesecake cheesecakes
coattail coattails	congresswoman congresswomen
fireman firemen	hatbox hatboxes
landscape landscapes	shoetree shoetrees
suitcase suitcases	teammate teammates
teapot teapots	teaspoon teaspoons

The last example brings us to an interesting consideration — **teaspoonful,** or *cupful* or *handful*. Is the plural *teaspoonfuls* or *teaspoonsful*? *Teaspoonfuls* is recognized as an acceptable plural because *teaspoonful* is a single entity: the quantity which can be held by a teaspoon. It is, however, awkward, and in spite of the argument that several *teaspoonsful* is equivalent, not to a measure, but to several teaspoons each full of something, it may be preferred. You have to decide.

Two word compound nouns are more fun. *Mother-in-law* becomes *mothers-in-law* because *mother* is the subject and *in-law* describes a relationship. The same principal applies to *editors-in-chief* and *ex-presidents*.

Notary public and *chairman of the board* offer a couple of unusual examples. The first is a *notary* who works in the public domain and a gathering of such men could be described as a group of *notaries public*; however, one might view the two words together as a title wherein each word carries equal weight in which case it would be a group of *notary publics*. *Attorney general* confronts us with the same logic so that either *attorneys general* or *attorney generals* is correct.

In the second example, a strong argument can be made that the gathered titans of industry are collectively *chairmen*, but of a like number of *boards* as each board has only one chairman. Thus we have a meeting of the *chairmen of the boards*. (Except for those boards which have co-chairmen). This is one of those places where there is no distinct right or wrong; we only hope that common sense will prevail and . . . you got it! . . . be consistent.

When there is no word in the compound that is clearly more important than the others, the plural is added at the end.

> **black-eyed Susan** black-eyed Susans
>
> **forget-me-not** forget-me-nots
>
> **jack-in the box** jack-in-the-boxes

In some cases, both parts of a compound should be plural.

> **manservant menservants**
>
> **woman lawyer** women lawyers

Minding your p's and q's

By this time you may be at 6's and 7's, but you should still be able to see where this rule is going with no if's, and's or but's. You have earned it; you deserve it: *an ironclad rule with no exceptions.*

The plural of a number, letter, word or symbol (+'s and *'s) is created by adding apostrophe *s*.

Nouns ending in -o

Nouns ending in *o* preceded by a consonant usually form the plural by adding *-es*.

hero heroes	**potato potatoes**	**tomato tomatoes**

There are, of course, exceptions to the rule,

dynamo dynamos	**photo photos**	**piano pianos**
silo silos	**solo solos**	**zero zeros**

including some words which form the plural either way.

cargo	**cargos**	**cargoes**
motto	**mottos**	**mottoes**
tornado	**tornados**	**tornadoes**

Nouns ending in *o* preceded by a vowel take an *s* only.

cameo cameo	**patio patios**	**radio radios**
trio trios	**zoo zoos**	

Proper nouns ending in *o* always take an *s* only.

Possessive plurals

Finally, another easy one. When you want to form the plural possessive, form the plural by the applicable rule (or exception) and if the word ends in an *s* add an apostrophe ('), otherwise add an apostrophe *s*.

ax	**axes**	**axes' handles**
brother	**brothers**	**brothers' share**
brother	**brethren**	**brethren's share**

child	children	children's toys
deer	deer	deer's grazing area
doctor	doctors	doctors' offices
man	men	men's room
mouse	mice	mice's holes
radius	radiuses	radiuses' lengths
radius	radii	redii's lengths
theory	theories	theories' premises
wife	wives	wives' tales
woman	women	women's lounge

And a serious note:

It may seem a waste of time to learn any rules of spelling when you consider all of the exceptions, but it's not. Most of the time when we need a little help it's simply a matter of being uncertain, and knowing the rules will often clear up that uncertainty. If it's a word we use often which is spelled contrary to the rules, we may look it up once and remember it for that very reason.

Hyphenation

Most grammarians have one bit of advice about hyphenation. Don't do it. As we deal with ever more sophisticated writing tools such as word processors and personal computers, we strive to turn out smarter looking documents which often require hyphenation.

Rather than get wrapped up in a lot of rules for hyphenation, follow just one: *use a dictionary and common sense.*

When a word is broken at the end of a line, make sure that enough of it is on the first line (at least three or four characters) to make a pronounceable syllable. If the eye can track without the necessity of pausing or rereading, your message loses impact. Similarly, a stack of hyphens where words have been broken on line after line makes tracking difficult.

Part IV
Form and Style

Form and Style

In spite of the disapproval of my several English instructors, all overworked, underpaid and most assuredly under appreciated, who even now are spinning in their graves, in is necessary to impart my own immutable **First Law of Grammar**, to wit:

> **Whereas the primary mission of language is to communicate,**
> > **and whereas nothing is writ in stone,**
> **Therefore, be it known that**
> > **although generally accepted usage is preferred,**
> **When generally accepted usage interferes with clarity**
> > **or is not up to the task at hand,**
> **Without hesitation or compunction, *Break the Rules*.**

The importance of style cannot be overemphasized. Everything you do reflects a style, good or bad. Whether the communication is spoken or written, the style influences the recipient as much as the message itself.

GENERAL CONSIDERATIONS

Formal or casual?

The dictionary describes *formal* as "**. . . in accordance with regular or established forms and methods, or with proper dignity.**" Taken liberally, that definition should fit virtually everything we write. It doesn't mean we have to be stuffy, nor does it mean we can't show a little creativity; it simply means that we do have to work within the confines of that which is acceptable to those who judge what we've written.

Some of the suggestions in this section may sound casual; rest assured, they are not. *Casual* means ". . . occurring by chance . . . haphazard . . .careless." To be any of those things is far from our intent. We will, however, direct your attention to communication in a style that is relaxed and unselfconscious, a technique which does not occur by chance.

First, you must assess the style which prevails in your present situation. If all of the correspondence you see is staid and very formal, find out why. Is it tradition, laziness on the part of the writers, your supervisor's preference or company policy? Determine how much latitude you have to communicate in a more relaxed, informative style. You may want to test the waters by changing outdated phrases to better reflect the way you speak before attempting any radical changes in the tone of correspondence.

Consistency

The tone of your correspondence is influenced by your assessment of the recipient: a relaxed note to a coworker; a formal. deferential letter to an officer of the company. The way in which you view your relationship to clients will affect the way in which you address them in your letters. Try to develop a style which is comfortable to you and which lends itself to every situation. A letter to an important (and perhaps, stuffy) client or an officer of the company does not have to be framed in archaic prose to be respectful. Aim for a consistent style, best expressed as the way you speak or would like to speak. Be the same person in a letter or a report that you are when talking on the phone.

Be consistent, also, in tendering accurate information in a timely manner. A problem-solving letter, even if it has only preliminary information is worth far more on the heels of the problem than after someone has had several days to stew about it.

Leave Your Imprint

Develop a style which reflects you. If possible, let the reader know you sent the letter before he or she reaches the signature line. Writing in a conversational manner will do it if all of the other correspondence your recipient gets is couched in formal, archaic language.

Form and style

You can also identify yourself by the greeting; the way in which you begin the letter; the letters you write because you care, not because you have to; the timeliness of your response; the way in which your relaxed style doesn't prevent you from getting to the point; the manner you have of summing up a problem, and the solution, concisely. All of these are discussed further in the section on **Business Letters**.

How to Offend the Recipient

Jab a sensitive nerve

Be relaxed, be friendly, but don't get too personal. The boss or client who refers jokingly to a spreading waistline or thinning hair is not extending an invitation to be ridiculed.

Jokes are fine, but be certain that they are in good taste. Whenever you are tempted to tell a story with racial, religious, sexual, etc. overtones or which may be offensive to the recipient, bite your tongue hard enough to make you yelp. Then you can change the subject, explaining that you bit your tongue.

Don't apologize

There is a conventional wisdom which holds that one should never open a letter with an apology. Poppycock! There are times when something goes wrong that a client or supervisor takes it personally and the first thing they want is an apology. There is, however, a right and wrong way.

A letter which begins by saying that you are sorry, but you don't know what happened and you hope it doesn't happen again is not going to be well received. An apology on a positive note, however, is another matter. Offering regrets that the incident occurred and that you are in the process of determining exactly what happened or are formulating a procedure to prevent recurrence is more likely to be well received. Continue by filling the recipient in on the status of your investigation or preliminary assessment of the situation. End with a promise to keep him or her informed and again offer regrets for any inconvenience you may have caused. Never mind that the client may have done something to create the problem; include that in your solution, not the finger pointing. He or she will get the message.

Any attempt to shift blame or avoid an apology to one who feels wronged will only feed the anger —don't do it unless that is your intent.

Mislead the recipient

You were told to do something, forgot it and a week later you're asked about it. Should you: (a) admit that you forgot; (b) suggest that your instructions may have been lost in the mail; (c) feign amnesia; or (d) claim you have a split personality and the message was given to your irresponsible half?

Misleading your recipient with vague or incorrect information is usually counter productive. It can cause a loss of confidence and at the very least engender a sense of frustration that *something* went wrong which neither of you can control.

Remember — it's not a life or death situation and the other person wants it to go away as much as you do. Owning up to a problem places the blame squarely on your shoulders. You get to be the recipient of someone else's frustration, but once vented, it's gone, and you can go on with your life. If you play your hand well, you may even wind up with a stronger relationship. Sure beats letting a problem fester while you squirm.

The Boss - the Final Arbiter

Any writing of consequence for most of us will be work or school related. The comments here are directed mainly to a work environment, but they apply equally well to school. The influence of the boss or a customer in the workplace is much the same as the instructor in school. For the student who thinks the pressure subsides when you got out into the real world — sorry about that. Nothing changes, except that hopefully you have the same boss for a lot longer than you have the same instructor.

Regardless of the influence, it affects your style. The degree to which you are subjected to influence, however, will vary tremendously from place to place. Though not very common, there are companies which have standards manuals for all written communication including channels of communication and a list of subjects which may (or may not) be communicated through those channels. Less structured, but certainly important, are the preferences of your immediate supervisor. He or she may have definite ideas about the configuration of written communication or may be pleased to avoid any involvement as long as you get the job done.

Guidelines for Effective Communication

Effective communication takes thought and planning

Develop a relaxed, comfortable style

Communicate in a timely manner

Be friendly without getting too personal

Apologize for errors, then offer a solution

Be direct and honest in what you have to say

DISTINCTIVE BUSINESS LETTERS

> **If the letter you are about to write is not important, don't write it. You're wasting your time, the time of the person who transcribes it and the time of the person who reads it.**

Many otherwise interesting people seem to find it easiest to write stiff, artificial, uninteresting letters. Please don't misunderstand. The business letter's primary purpose is not to entertain, but it shouldn't put the reader to sleep, either.

The unstated message

The business letter carries more than the stated message; it carries a message about the writer and the way in which he or she conducts business. To get the most out of a letter, be sure that the *unstated message* is acceptable.

How do you regard the recipient? Do you think enough of the person to whom you are sending the letter to spell his or her name right? The business which relies on a word processor or computer has a distinct advantage — check the name carefully once, when it's put into the system, and it will come out correctly thereafter. Anyone who lacks this convenience is well advised to take a few seconds to be sure the name is correct every time. And don't rely entirely someone else who transcribed the letter; he or she may be very reliable, but the blame for any mistakes rests with you. The same is true for titles. Some people are very protective of theirs and you should be too. If there is any doubt about the spelling of a name or the wording of a title, taking a couple of minutes to call the person's office to confirm is good investment.

How do you regard the recipient's company? For most people, the company is an important part of their lives. They need to know that you respect their employer. Be sure the name is spelled correctly, and **put it in capital letters**.

How do you regard your message? Is it important enough to spell out clearly in a neat, well-fashioned letter? In this age of computers and word processors where erasures do not exist, the erasures in a letter prepared on a typewriter stand out more than at any time in the past and thus it is far more important to avoid them.

How competent are you? A sloppy letter, full of errors, written by someone who rambles and seems to have difficulty expressing himself or herself is not likely to engender confidence in the recipient.

Body of the letter

Grabber greetings

You have just a few seconds to make sure that the reader is alert to receive your message. An out-of-the-ordinary opening will do the trick. Dear So-and-so is fine, but why not change occasionally to show that it's not automatic?

> **Good morning, Ms. Jones.**
>
> **Good afternoon, Mr. Smith.**
>
> **Congratulations, Shirley.**

Or you can dive right in.

> **Just received your letter, Sam,**
> **and we're really pleased that you decided . . .**
>
> **How did you manage, Rosemary,**
> **to pull off the deal they said couldn't be done?**

The trick is to write the first sentence and then rework it, if necessary, to include the recipients name in the sentence.

Write the way you speak

The best way to give the reader a message which is distinctively you is to write the way you talk. Stiff, precise language in a letter is not wrong, it's just boring. If we want our letters to be remembered when others are forgotten, we need to be distinctive and writing in a conversational manner is one of the tools we have to make our communication memorable.

Obviously we can't include all of the pauses and hand gestures and facial expressions that are a part of face to face conversation, but we can adopt a conversational tone. Use short sentences and even phrases if they help make a point. Avoid overly long compound-complex sentences, if possible. Above all, avoid officious language which you are not likely to use when speaking.

> **as per your letter** — legalese; use *according to your letter*
>
> **attached please find, enclosed please find** — just say *attached is* or *enclosed is*
>
> **at the present time** — most of us say *now*
>
> **contents noted** — outdated
>
> **in compliance with your request** — as you requested
>
> **in receipt of your letter, in response to your letter** — of course you received the letter; why else would you be responding?
>
> **in the amount of** — use *for $_____*
>
> **please advise when** — How about *inform me*, or *tell me* or *let me know when*?
>
> **please arrange to return** — use *return* or *send*
>
> **pursuant to your instructions** — use *per your instructions* or *as you requested*
>
> **we are desirous of receiving** — *we would like* or *please send*

Be bright, be brief and be gone

An old adage for salesmen, it applies equally well to business letters: know what you want to talk about; say it concisely; stop and go away. There's always room for a personal comment when appropriate, but don't abuse it by rambling on needlessly. It does not make friends.

Types of business letters

Introductory letters

An introductory letter is any letter written to an unknown party to introduce the writer as a job applicant, a possible supplier of goods or services, etc. These are without doubt the toughest letters to write because you are writing to someone who not only doesn't know you, but doesn't have any reason to want to know you. And you usually don't know enough about the person to whom you are writing to customize the letter. You have only a slight chance the letter will even be read by the person to whom it is addressed. Most people who send out blind letters plan to send a lot of them in the hope of a few responses.

If you have some knowledge of the person you are trying to reach you may be able to tailor the letter in a way that improves your chance for response. The best way is to offer a service which the company needs and does not have available through current suppliers.

You can improve your chances with a clever opener, but not so clever that the letter gets tossed out with the occupant mailings. Once you've garnered attention with the opener, state your business briefly and ask for a response. Don't try to sell yourself or your entire line of products in that one shot; your goal is a response which will get you an appointment or a request for more information.

If you know something about the company, you might write a letter praising a product or a community project in which the company is involved. Well into the body of the letter, or even in a following letter, you mention that you would like to be associated with the company as an employee or a supplier.

In addition to asking for a response, some situations lend themselves to a follow-up call in which case you might indicate in the letter that you will call in a few days to arrange an appointment, answer any questions, etc.

Answering inquiries

It is extremely important that inquiries be answered as completely as possible, in a timely manner and scheduled for follow-up.

The response to an inquiry requires the same planning as any letter. The old *Dear-sir-thank-you-for-your-inquiry-here's-the-stuff-you-requested* letter doesn't cut it. The response needs to be personal, friendly and inviting further contact. Based on the type of inquiry, it may be prudent to include additional information. A follow-up call or letter is in order to be sure that the material received is satisfactory.

Orders

Orders keep the business going and repeat orders are the most inexpensive source of new business. Orders should be followed immediately with a friendly letter expressing thanks for the order, expressing confidence that the customer will be pleased and inviting a call if there are any questions or problems. In addition, it may be appropriate to convey additional information such as ship date, routing, etc. as well as a reminder of other products which may be of interest.

Follow-up

Use of the computer makes it easier than it has ever been to track our business activity. We can log in the dates when introductory letters were sent and to whom; when inquiries were answered; when orders were placed by product line and quantity. The allows for a very efficient follow-up system.

In addition to follow-up letters for inquiries and orders, we can schedule letters to go out when we think a client is getting low on product. The letter may be a friendly reminder that it is time to check inventory or it may simply be a request for assurance that the customer is happy with the product.

We can also inform clients any time we have a special buy on the particular product which they use or related products which they may use.

Good will letters

Good will letters are those you write because you care. Congratulations on a promotion or recognition of a personal achievement is just one more opportunity to keep in touch. Condolences on the loss of a loved one is a means to let the client know you care. Needless to say, these are brief business letters wherein no business is discussed.

Interoffice

Interoffice correspondence deserves the same care that outside correspondence receives. Interoffice may be more cryptic and in some cases more technical, but the admonition to write well should not be ignored. Whether writing to a superior or your peers, you face the same job of convincing them to agree with your requests.

Guidelines for Effective Business Letters

Rely on the appearance of the letter to create a favorable impression

Avoid conventional openings and hackneyed phrases

Write the way you speak

Be concise; say what you have to say, then stop

Use correspondence to develop and maintain a relationship

Don't underestimate the importance of interoffice communication

---

REPORTS

Probably the main difference between an academic and a business report is the manner in which the subject is selected — the student is usually required to select his own subject, whereas in the workplace there is a specific problem to be addressed. For this example, we'll use a hypothetical business problem.

Define the problem

Describing the problem properly is often the key to finding a solution.

The ABC Company

The ABC Company is a small company in the midwest which manufactures microwave ovens. Recently they have experienced a rash of complaints about damaged product manufactured exclusively for a large retailer. The rate is high — five to ten per cent in some cases — and in addition to the cost of returns, the Sales Department is concerned about a loss of customer confidence in the company's other products.

The problem

The problem seems simple enough — defective units are being shipped to a customer. But that description is too broad to help define a precise solution. The precise problem may involve inferior materials, poor workmanship, inadequate inspection, careless handling, etc. More information is needed to properly define the problem and outline remedial action.

Assemble the facts

Quality control — The Quality Control Department, which is responsible for inspecting the returned units, reports that the same part is broken on most of the units inspected. They also report that the parts are 100% inspected at the end of the assembly line.

Packing and shipping — The Shipping Department, which is also responsible for packing, reports that packing and shipping is the same as for other products which have had no damage reported.

Freight forwarder — The freight company confirms that the damaged units travel many of the same routes as, and often side by side with, units which have a history of no damage claims.

Purchasing — The Purchasing Department produces documentation to show that all materials purchased for the damaged units meet engineering specifications; however, they note that the packing material specifications call for a lighter material than that used for other products.

Suppliers — Supplier of the packing material confirms that a lighter material is used, but that it was tested and proved adequate for this lighter product.

Sales — After Engineering pointed the finger, Sales confirmed that the lighter material was specified to comply with the customer's request for a smaller over-all package size.

Customer — The customer confirms that the smaller package was requested in order to maximize the number of pieces they could pack in their warehouse units. Inspection of the customer's facility revealed that they re-piled the units on special pallets with all identification labels facing one way and stacked them higher than they were on the shipping pallet.

Engineering — Experimenting with the customer's warehouse packing, the Engineering Department determined that the packing is inadequate. The units are much heavier on one side, and so it is standard practice at the plant to alternate the packages when piling to distribute the weight. Turning the packages all one way puts too much stress on the lower packages. They also determined that the part which most often failed was a very tight fit which made it more susceptible to the extra pressure.

Redefine the problem

Based on the information compiled the problem might be defined as — **The stress placed on the package by the customer's warehousing methods which causes frequent failure of part X.**

Outline the options

Outlining the options means considering every possibility, regardless of how bizarre and establishing a cost for it.

Sometimes the outrageous leads to a simpler, though less obvious, solution. Remember the story of the man who went to his doctor and said, "Doc, it hurts when I do this," and the doctor said, "Don't do that." Your first option might be to stop making the unit. The cost of that decision is lost profits, possible loss of prestige and loss of position in the market place.

Among other options are strengthening the packaging, strengthening the part, redesign of the product, labeling both sides of the package coupled with educating the customer in the best way to re-stack, stacking at the plant on the customer's pallets so that re-stacking isn't necessary, etc.

In every case, consider the cost in dollars and the need for agreement of the parties involved in the change.

Suggest a solution

Usually, when the options are outlined, an obvious solution presents itself; however, the interest of all parties must be considered, so that it may be necessary to outline more than one choice.

Put it all together

What we have outlined is a problem solving technique, although most reports follow the same pattern. Any report which is not merely a statistical summary may imply an evaluation which requires research of fact and opinion regarding the subject.

In the summation, every report requires a heading which states the problem or objective, a brief summary of the pertinent facts, a list of the reasonable options and a detailed description of the recommended action including costs, penalties, potential problems, etc.

Key Elements in a Report

State the problem or purpose

Summarize the pertinent facts

Outline the options with their cost

Recommend a solution

PUBLIC SPEAKING

So you've been asked to give a speech. Or perhaps, like many of us, it came as an imperial command; the boss was asked to give a speech and doesn't want to do it, so he volunteered you. Either way, the subject matter was probably chosen for you, whether it's outlining the activities of your department for a group of fellow employees, telling the company story to a local civic group or describing a special process to a professional group.

The steps to planning and delivering a speech are not so difficult, but they do take a little time. Hopefully, you've been given enough notice to plan, research and run through the speech a few times before delivering it.

Relate the subject to the audience

Based on the length of the speech and the audience, you have to decide whether the subject matter should be technical or an overview, instructional or entertaining.

Research

Surely you are familiar with the subject or you wouldn't have been asked to speak, but you probably want to seek additional information. Scan through any books, reports, etc. you can find for facts to fill out what you already know and for new information. Don't worry about finding too much material; it's easier to cull out the excess than to try to stretch too little. The more you know, the more comfortable you will be with your subject.

In addition, interview anyone who knows anything about the subject. Transfer all of your notes to 3x5 cards referencing the source.

Form and style

Anecdotes

One of the benefits of interviews is that they are a great source of anecdotes which can be used to liven up or change the pace of the speech. Make notes of anecdotes and withhold judgment about their use until you organize your presentation.

Plan the presentation

Flow

By now you should have a collection of note cards from your research. Supplement these with cards noting information and anecdotes drawn from your own experience.

If you have a general outline of the ground you plan to cover, sort the note cards under the various headings.

If you don't have an outline, use the notes to build one. Spread them out on a desk or table and put them in the order you feel they should be introduced. Identify any notes which might be a main heading or section of the presentation and isolate the cards which belong to that group. Create a heading for any group of notes which seem to fit in the same section and keep those together.

Review the outline to see that the information flows in a logical sequence. If not, make any necessary changes. A presentation which flows in an orderly fashion and is broken down into segments will not only be easier to for the listener to follow, but easier for you to deliver. In all likelihood, you will change the outline again before you're through, but this is a start.

Pacing

Review the outline again to critically assess the content of each section. Is there any way a section can be punched up with an anecdote or side comment? Do you want to consider the use of charts or graphs to better illustrate a point? Are there comparisons which you might use to make a point more dramatic?

All of this is part of the pacing. Standing in front of a room, reciting cold, hard facts while clinging to a podium until your knuckles are white is not only unnerving to the audience, it is likely to be unnerving to you. Anything you can do to change the pace in a natural manner is going to be more comfortable for everyone.

Length

There's no way to know exactly how long the speech will be until you have run through it a couple of times, but at this point you can probably make a good guess. Review the outline again and make some judgment about things which might be added or eliminated to correct the length.

Cue cards and props

Only you can determine what sort of notes you need on the podium. Some people are only comfortable with the speech written out in full, others use an outline, still others list only the main sections. One popular speaker years ago carried 3x5 cards in his left hand and referred to them occasionally when he spoke. They were blank! a prop to help him along.

A prop such as a chart or graph can help if it has written on it the key words you need as a guide; or it can be positioned on an easel in front of you with an outline on the back visible only to you.

Whatever method you choose, you may well change it as you practice the speech. Sometimes the information flows so well that a few key words is all you need. On the other hand, you may need the security of a typed copy of the full speech in front of you.

One word of caution — if there are any direct quotes in your speech, write them out on 3x5 cards, just in case. You may be able to talk about your company all day without a problem, but nothing could be more embarrassing than to forget the president's words or his name at a critical moment.

Practice, practice, practice

Avoid the temptation to write out the entire speech. You and your audience will both be more comfortable if you maintain a conversational style. Think of the speech in that way: as a conversation with a group of friends.

Dry run

Not until you run through the speech will you know exactly how long it is. And the first run-through is full of surprises.

This is when you discover that half of your outline contains one-liners: facts about the company which are stated in simple sentences and don't lend themselves to any embellishment. Your thirty minute speech could be barely fifteen minutes. Or when you realize that the process which is so familiar to you defies description in non-technical jargon.

To make matters worse, the material just doesn't seem to flow, and you have to revise the outline. Basically, this is when you work the hardest and sweat the most to pull it all together. But you do pull it all together.

Once the initial hurdles are past, run through the speech again to be sure that the material flows well and that the speech is about the right length.

Segment the presentation

Begin to view the speech as several small speeches. Divide it into segments according to your outline. Run through the segments individually until you are comfortable with them.

As you grow more comfortable with what you have to say, practice in front of a mirror so that you can see what your audience will see. Take a deep breath and look around the room before you begin. Speak slowly at first. Criticize your own performance and if you find it boring, try to be more animated without overdoing it. Change the volume, pitch and pace of your words when appropriate, just as you would in normal conversation. Above all, relax.

Final Notes

Prepare the notes that you will take with you: key words, outline or full text as well as copies of any direct quotations or statistics.

Now run through from beginning to end with only that material in front of you. You're ready!

Two more pieces of advice: Be sure you have a glass of water handy because even if you are not nervous, all that talking can give you a dry mouth. Don't open with a joke unless it's appropriate and a sure thing; starting out with a bomb can be devastating to you and your audience. Better to scatter some light humor through your presentation. Now, *that* can hold an audience.

Follow these rules and you will be so successful that the only thing you have to worry about is overconfidence which will keep you from working as hard on your next speech.

Guidelines for Effective Speaking

Know your subject well

Speak in terms your audience can understand

Vary the pace of the presentation with anecdotes or props

Keep final notes to a minimum

Practice until you are at ease telling your story

Keep a written copy of quotes or critical statistics

Relax, you're talking to friends

Part V
Reference

REFERENCE

CONFUSING WORDS

In spelling and in speaking, we are plagued by words which are, in some cases, so similar in spelling or meaning that we don't even suspect we are using a wrong word or that there is any difference between two words. Following is a list and explanation of the most common offenders.

accept, except *Accept* means to receive — *to accept a package;* to agree to — *to accept a decision;* to acknowledge — *to accept an invitation. Except* means to leave out — *No one is excepted from the restrictions* or *Take them all except the blue ones.*

adapt, adopt *Adapt* means to modify or make suitable — *to adapt to one's surroundings. Adopt* means to take as one's own — *to adopt an idea; to vote to adopt a resolution; to adopt a child.*

addition, edition *Addition* is the process of joining together or finding the sum of. *Edition* is the published form of a literary work — *de luxe edition* or *first edition;* total number of copies issued at one time — *an edition of 20,000.*

adopt See **adapt**

advice, advise *Advice* (soft *c* pronounced like an *s*) is a noun — *to give advice to a person. Advise* (hard *s* pronounce like a *z*) is a verb — *to advise a person.*

affect, effect *Affect* means to influence or act upon — *this won't affect you. Effect,* as a verb, means to bring about, to cause — *the treatments will effect a swift cure;* as a noun, means the result or outcome — *that is the effect of the treatment.*

aisle, isle *Aisle* is a passageway between seats in a church or theater. *Isle* is a small island.

186

Reference

alley, ally *Alley* is a narrow passageway between or behind buildings; a lane for bowling. *Ally* means to unite or enter into an alliance; an associate or helper.

all ready, already *All ready* (always two words) means that everyone is prepared — *We are all ready to go. Already* refers to a past time or by this time or by the time mentioned — *That has already been done.*

all right, alright *All right* is the correct spelling — *Everything is all right. Alright* is used mainly as an interjection in a narrative and is not considered acceptable for use in general correspondence — *"Alright, I'll go!"*

all together, altogether *All together* implies several acting in unison — *We must go all together,* or *All together now, sing! Altogether* represents a whole or the entirety — *This is altogether too much.*

allude, elude *Allude* means to make indirect or casual reference — *She alluded to his unkind remarks. Elude* means to avoid or escape — *The meaning of that word eludes me.*

ally See **alley**

already See **all ready**

altar, alter *Altar* is a raised table or platform which is the focal point of a place of worship. *Alter* means to change or modify.

altogether See **all together**

among, between *Among* is used to refer to more than two. *Between* usually refers to only two, but there are exceptions. See also **Prepositions, Words to watch.**

angel, angle *Angel* is a spiritual being. *Angle* is a geometric value formed by the joining of two lines.

appraise, apprise *Appraise* means to make an official evaluation — *He must appraise the property before we can set a price. Apprise* means to notify or inform — *Be sure to apprise her of our decision.*

ascent, assent *Ascent* means rising or climbing — *the ascent of the mountain* (by someone), *the ascent of the group up the mountain, the ascent of the plane into the heavens. Assent* means agreement or consent — *to assent to the course of action.*

bare, bear *Bare* means devoid of any covering. *Bear* means to support or hold up — *Can you bear the burden?*; a large mammal that lives in the woods.

baring, barring, bearing *Baring* means to uncover — *baring a secret. Barring* means apart from, excepting — *Barring traffic, we'll be there shortly. Bearing* means deportment, manner of carrying oneself — *a person of regal bearing;* endurance — *bearing up under pressure.*

between See **among**

born, borne, bourn *Born* means to be brought into being, as an offspring. *Borne* is the past participle of bear — *to have borne the load. Bourn* means that which limits, goal, end — *the bourn of one's life.*

breath, breathe *Breath* (pronounced with a short *e*) is a noun which means air inhaled or exhaled; a soft movement of air. *Breathe* (pronounced with a long *e*) is a verb which means to inhale or exhale; to whisper — *don't breathe a word to anyone.*

can, may *Can* expresses ability to do something — *You can* (are able to) *drive the car. May* expresses permission — *You may* (are allowed to) *drive the car.*

canvas, canvass *Canvas* describes a cloth used for sails, tents, etc.; a painting. *Canvass* is to go about soliciting orders, votes, etc.; a survey to determine preference.

capital, capitol *Capital* refers to something standing at the head or beginning: wealth used to make more wealth — *a capital investment;* the chief city of an area, usually the seat of government — *Atlanta is the capital of Georgia;* the first letter in a sentence — *a capital letter;* the member or section at the top of a column. *Capitol* refers to the building in which a legislature meets.

censor, censure *Censor*, as a noun, describes the official who examines material to be judged for rating, acceptability, etc. — *the censor has to see the material first;* as a verb, describes the act of deleting or suppressing material — *some of the best parts have been censored. Censure,* as a verb, is to express disapproval — *he was censured by his teammates for his conduct;* as a noun, is a formal reprimand expressing disapproval and which may include other discipline, punishment or forfeiture — *Censure was his only punishment.*

census, senses *Census* is an official count of the people of a country, area, etc. *Senses* (plural of *sense*) is a reference to awareness or rationality — *to come to your senses.*

cite, sight, site *Cite* means to quote or to call up as an authority or example — *to cite the words of Plato* or *to cite the instance when . . . . Sight* is the faculty of seeing — *my sight is fine;* a vision — *such a beautiful sight. Site* is a location — *the site of the battle.*

clothes, cloths *Clothes* are garments. *Cloths* is the plural of *cloth*, a piece of fabric.

complement, compliment A *complement* is that which fills up or completes — *The ship has her full complement of hands.* A *compliment* is praise — *I must compliment you on a delightful party.*

consul, council, counsel A *consul* is an officer residing in a foreign country to protect his country's interests. A *council* is an assemblage convened for consultation — *The Security Council is meeting today. Counsel* is guidance or advice — *She can counsel you on the proper steps to take;* a lawyer — *we sought the advice of counsel.*

corps, corpse A *corps* (pronounce like the core of an apple) is a military unit. A *corpse* is a dead body.

costume, custom *Costume* refers to apparel. *Custom* refers to common usage or practice.

credible, creditable *Credible* means worthy of being believed — *a credible story. Creditable* describes something worthy of praise — *The team made a creditable showing.*

custom See **costume**

dairy, diary A *dairy* is a place where milk products are processed and sold. A *diary* is a record of daily events.

decent, descent, dissent *Decent* means proper or respectable — *They are decent people. Descent* is the act of going downward — *We shall begin our descent shortly. Dissent*, as a verb, means to disagree — *I must dissent from your analysis;* as a noun, means a disagreement — *There is dissent among the people.*

desert, dessert *Desert* refers to a barren land; that which is deserved or merited — *his just deserts* ; to abandon. *Dessert* is something sweet served after a meal.

device, devise A *device* is a contrivance — *This device will allow you to save money heating your home. Devise* means to invent or contrive — *We have devised a plan for achieving our goals.*

diary See **dairy**

dissent See **decent**

dual, duel *Dual* denotes two. A *duel* refers to a struggle between two parties.

edition See **addition**

effect See **affect**

effective, effectual *Effective* means to produce a desired result — *The cost-cut-*

ting measures have been effective; in force, referring to a rule or law — *These new regulations are effective immediately. Effectual* means having the power to produce a desired result — *We can cut our costs by adopting effectual procedures.*

elicit, illicit *Elicit* is to draw out, as by inducement — *to elicit the truth. Illicit* describes a thing as unlawful or unauthorized.

elude See **allude**

eminent, imminent *Eminent* refers to one who is high in station, distinguished or prominent — *an eminent scientist. Imminent* describes something as about to happen, usually said of danger or evil — *The failure of the company is imminent.*

except See **accept**

formally, formerly *Formally* means in a formal manner — *to be greeted formally* or *to be formally attired. Formerly* refers to some time in the past — *Formerly, she was a lawyer.*

forth, fourth *Forth* indicates forward. *Fourth* refers to one of four equal parts; number four in succession.

gamble, gambol To *gamble* is to take a chance. *Gambol* is to play or frolic.

holly, holy, wholly *Holly* is a plant. *Holy* means to be hallowed or consecrated. *Wholly* means entirely.

hoping, hopping *Hoping* refers to desire. *Hopping* is moving about in short leaps.

illicit See **elicit**

imminent See **eminent**

instance, instants *Instance* refers to an occurrence as an illustration or example. *Instants* is the plural of *instant*, a particular point in time.

isle See **aisle**

lay, lie *Lay*, in the present tense, means to put or place — *Lay the book on the table*; as the past tense of lie, means to recline — *This morning, he was so tired, he had to lay* (not laid) *down. Lie* means to recline (present tense) — *Lie* (not lay) *down on the couch.*

learn, teach To *learn* is to acquire knowledge. To *teach* is to impart knowledge. The teacher teaches; the student learns.

lessen, lesson *Lessen* means to make less or decrease — *to lessen the work load. Lesson* is that which is learned or to be learned — *study tomorrow's lesson.*

loath, loathe *Loath* is an adjective which expresses reluctance — *He was loath to do the deed. Loathe* is a verb which expresses hatred or disgust — *I loathe the smell of the chemical plant.*

loose, lose *Loose* means not tight or not fastened — *a loose fit* or *on the loose. Lose* means to mislay or be deprived of — *to lose the book* or *to lose a privilege.*

may See **can**

medal, metal A *medal* is a small metal symbol, usually conferred for special achievement. *Metal* refers to a hard element or alloy.

morn, mourn *Morn* is a poetic term for morning. *Mourn* means to express sorrow or grief.

passed, past *Passed*, as a verb (past tense and past participle of pass), means to have gone by or left behind — *The car passed us on the road*; as an adjective, means to successfully complete an examination — *We passed the test. Past*, as an adjective, indicates that which is accomplished or ended — *our past achievements*; as a noun, refers to time gone by — *our sins of the past*; as a preposition, means beyond in time or place beyond — *The car went past us* or *it is past noon.*

peace, piece *Peace* is a state of tranquility; the absence of war. *Piece* is a portion or part of a greater whole.

persecute, prosecute *Persecute* is to harass or annoy consistently, especially because of race, religion or opinions. *Prosecute* is usually used in the legal sense and means to bring suit against.

personal, personnel *Personal* refers to an individual — *a personal matter* or *personal opinion. Personnel* refers to a group of people — *company personnel* or *the personnel department.*

piece See **peace**

plain, plane *Plain* means to be flat or smooth; to be unadorned; level, treeless land. A *plane* is a flat surface; a stage of development; an airplane; a tool for smoothing wood.

practicable, practical *Practicable* refers to that which is anticipated to be feasible or usable — *a practicable idea. Practical* pertains to actual use or experience — *a practical solution.*

precede, proceed *Precede* means to go before in order — *Dinner will precede the speeches. Proceed* means to go forward or to continue — *After a rest, we will proceed.*

precedence, precedents *Precedence* implies priority — *Education should take*

191

precedence over defense spending in the new budget. Precedents is the plural of *precedent,* which describes previous or established procedure — *The case may be strengthened by citing precedents established in previous court rulings.*

presence, presents *Presence* is the state of being in attendance — *Your presence is requested at the meeting. Presents* are the gifts you give and receive.

principal, principle *Principal* means to be first in rank or importance — *She is to be the principal speaker. Principle* refers to a general truth or law — *the principle of a representative government;* moral standards collectively — *He is a man of principle.*

prosecute See **persecute**

quiet, quite *Quiet* refers to a state of calm or tranquility. *Quite* is an adverb which expresses absolute certainty, without reservation — *He is quite dead.*

rain, reign, rein *Rain* is a weather condition. To *reign* is to rule. *Rein* describes a strap to control an animal; the act of checking or halting — *get a rein on the outrageous spending.*

right, rite, write *Right* describes that which is accurate, correct, or true. A *rite* is a ceremony. To *write* is to compose or create; to commit to paper.

senses See **census**

serf, surf A *serf* is a peasant attached to the land. The *surf* is the swell of the sea breaking against land.

shone, shown *Shone* is the past tense and past participle of *shine. Shown* is the past participle of *show.*

sight See **cite**

site See **cite**

sole, soul *Sole* means only. *Soul* represents the vital as opposed to the physical characteristics of a person or thing; the moral or spiritual part of a person.

staid, stayed *Staid* describes a steady or sedate manner. *Stayed,* the past tense of *stay,* means stopped, remained or ceased.

stake, steak *Stake* is a pointed stick of wood. *Steak* is a piece of meat.

stationary, stationery *Stationary* refers to office supplies. *Stationery* means to be fixed in place.

stayed See **staid**

steak See **stake**

steal, steel *Steal* is to take without authority; to move stealthily. *Steel* is an alloy compound of iron; to make strong or unyielding — *to steel one's self against trouble.*

suite, sweet *Sweet* is a taste like sugar. A *suite* is a set of things which are intended to be used together —*a suite of offices* or a *bedroom suite* (furniture).

surf See **serf**

teach See **learn**

than, then *Than* is a conjunction which expresses comparison — *She is taller than you are. Then* usually denotes *at that time* — *We were young then;* or expresses relative time — *Wash the dishes, then take out the garbage;* as a conjunction, it means as a consequence —*I will do it then, since you won't.*

their, there, they're *Their* is the possessive of *they* — *their house. There* indicates a place away from the speaker — *It is over there. They're* is the contraction of *they are* — *they're going to do it.*

wander, wonder *Wander* is to roam about. *Wonder* is a feeling of surprise and curiosity.

weak, week *Weak* is to lack strength. *Week* is a period of seven days.

weather, whether *Weather* refers to the condition of the atmosphere; to pass through and survive, as a crisis. *Whether* introduces or implies an alternative —*whether (or not) you are going.*

wholly See **holly**

who's, whose *Who's* is the contraction of *who is* — *Who's going? Whose* is the possessive of *who* — *Whose sweater is this?*

write See **right**

your, you're *Your* is the possessive of *you* — *Is this your sweater? You're* is the contraction of *you are* — *You're going?*

ABBREVIATIONS

The abbreviation is a convenient form which should be used with discretion and a modicum of judgment.

In general, they are not used in the body of correspondence except for titles, certain literary or technical terms and acronyms.

Be sure that any abbreviations you use, particularly of a technical nature are familiar to your reader.

When in doubt about the use of an abbreviation, don't use it.

Personal names and titles

Given names are not abbreviated except in the accepted form of a company name

Geo. W. Smith & Sons, Inc.

or on the signature line of a letter, if that is the author's preference.

Titles before a name are usually abbreviated except that civil or military titles are spelled out when used with the last name only.

Mr. John J. Smith or **Mr. Smith**

Gen. Mark Clark or **General Clark**

Sen. Hubert H. Humphrey or **Senator Humphrey**

Titles, degrees, affiliations, etc. after a name are abbreviated after a full name and are not used after the last name only.

The title, etc. after a name is set off with a comma except for II, III, 2d or 3d denoting succession.

James A. Kingston, Jr.   **James A. Kingston II**

The title esquire (Esq.) is not used with another title, before or after a name.

Organizations

Abbreviations in the name of an organization should follow the form used by the organization on its letterhead. The same is true of an acronym for the organizational name. When writing about an organization to a third party, be sure that any acronyms are familiar to the reader.

Commonly used abbreviations and acronyms are contained in the list of abbreviations on the following pages.

Place names

Abbreviations in street addresses may be written with or without periods.

City, state and zip codes should be separated by spaces without punctuation. The postal abbreviations for state names are included on the following pages.

Names of places, monuments, historic sites, etc. should be written out whenever possible to avoid confusion.

Measure and time

Despite the admonition to avoid abbreviations in text, it is not always practical to do so. The only recourse is to use good judgment to create a document which looks attractive, is easy to read and will be understood by the reader.

It can be awkward if the same terms need to be used a number of times when describing size or capacity. In such cases, abbreviations are preferred in the interest of brevity and clarity.

The days of the week and the months of the year are commonly abbreviated, however, spelling them out is preferred. The times of day, A.M. or P.M., are always abbreviated and may be lower case as well.

Commercial, scholarly and technical

Each endeavor has its own language with terms familiar only to those who take part. Just as care should be taken to avoid technical terms when addressing someone not familiar with the terms, far more care should be taken to avoid abbreviations which may be misunderstood.

A

a. about

AA Alcoholics Anonymous, author's alterations

AAA or **A.A.A.** Amateur Athletic Association, American Automobile Association, Automobile Association of America

AARP American Association of Retired Persons

A.A.U. Amateur Athletic Union

A.A.U.P. American Association of University Professors

A.A.U.W. American Association of University Women

A.B. Bachelor of Arts (Latin *Artium Baccalaureus*)

ABA American Bar Association, American Booksellers Association

abbr. or **abbrev.** abbreviation

abr. abridged, abridgment

abs. absent, absolute(ly) 3 abstract

a,/c or **A/C** account, account current

Ac *chem.* actinium

AC or **A.C.** or **a.c.** *electr.* alternating current

A.C. After Christ., Athletic Club

acad. academic, academy

acc. account, *gram.* accusative

accel. *music* accelerando, accelerate

acct. account, accountant

accus. *gram.* accusative

ack. acknowledge, acknowledgment

ACLU American Civil Liberties Union

ACS or **A.C.S.** American Chemical Society

A/cs Pay. accounts payable

A/cs Rec. accounts receivable

actg. acting

A.D. In the year of our Lord (Latin *anno domini*)

A.D.A. American Dental Association, Americans for Democratic Action

add. addenda, addendum., addition., address

ad fin. at, to, or toward the end (Latin *ad finem*)

adj. adjacent, adjective, adjunct

adm. administrative, administrator

Adm. Admiral

admin. administration, administrator

adv. in proportion (Latin *ad valorem*), *gram.* adverb, adverbial, advertisement

advt. advertisement

A.E.A. Actors' Equity Association

aeron. aeronautic, aeronautics

AFL or **A.F.L.** or **A.F. of L.** American Federation of Labor

AFL-CIO or **A.F.L.-C.I.O.** American Federation of Labor and the Congress of Industrial Organizations

Ag *chem.* Silver (Latin *argentum*)

A.G. Attorney General

agcy. agency

agr. agricultural, agriculture, agriculturist

AK Alaska

aka also known as

AKC or **A.K.C.** American Kennel Club

Al *chem.* aluminum

AL Alabama

Ald. or, as title, **Aldm.** alderman

alg. *math.* algebra

alt. alternate, alternating, alternative, alteration(s), altitude, *music* alto

alter. alteration

alum. aluminum

am. ammeter

Am *chem.* americium

Am. America, American

A.M. Master of Arts (Latin Artium Magister)

A.M. or **a.m.** *ante meridiem*, before noon.

AMA or **A.M.A.** American Management Association, American Medical Association

Amb. ambassador

Amer. America, American.

Am. Ind. American Indian.

amp. *electr.* amperage, ampere(s)

amp.-hr. *electr.* ampere-hour

amt. amount

anat. anatomical, anatomist, anatomy

and. *music* andante

Angl. Anglican, Anglicized

anim. animated, *music* animato

anon. anonymous

ans. answer, answered.

ant. antenna, antiquarian, antiquity, antonym

antilog. antilogarithm

antiq. antiquarian, antiquities

ap. apothecaries' (weight or measure)

approx. approximately

Apr. April

apt. (*pl.* **apts.**) apartment

Ar *chem.* argon

AR Arkansas

arch. archaic, archaism, architect, architectural, architecture.

archeol. archeology

archit. architecture

arg. silver (Latin *argentum*)

197

arith. arithmetic(al)

ARM adjustable-rate mortgage

Armen. Armenian

arr. arrange, arranged, arrangement(s), arrival, arrive, arrived

art. article

As *chem.* arsenic

ASA or **A.S.A.** American Standards Association

asb. asbestos

ASCAP or **A.S.C.A.P.** American Society of Composers, Authors and Publishers

A.S.P.C.A. American Society for the Prevention of Cruelty to Animals

assd. assigned

assn. association

assoc. associate, association

asst. assistant

astrol. astrologer, astrological, astrology

astron. astronomer, astronomical, astronomy

At *chem.* astatine

athl. athlete, athletic, athletics

atm. *physics* atmosphere, atmospheric

att. attention, attorney

atten. attention

attn. attention

attrib. attribute, attributive

atty. attorney

Atty. Gen. Attorney General

Au *chem.* gold (Latin *aurum*)

aud. audible, audit, auditor

Aug. August

auth. author, authority, authorized

auto. automatic, automotive

aux. or **auxil.** auxiliary

avdp. avoirdupois

ave. avenue

avg. average

avn. aviation

avoir. avoirdupois

AZ Arizona

az. azimuth

B

B *chem.* boron

Ba *chem.* barium

B.A. Bachelor of Arts (Latin *Baccalaureus Artium*)

bact. bacteriological, bacteriology.

bal. balance, balancing

bar. barometer, barometric

barit. *music* baritone

BASIC Beginner's All-purpose Symbolic Instruction Code

BBC or **B.B.C.** British Broadcasting Corporation

bbl. (*pl.* **bbls.**) barrel

B.C. Before Christ

BCD binary coded decimal

bd. (*pl.* **bds.**) board, bond

bd. ft. board feet.

bdl. bundle

Be *chem.* beryllium

bf or **b. f.** *printing* bold face

B/F brought forward

bg. (*pl.* **bgs.**) bag

Bi *chem.* bismuth

bibl. bibliographical

bibliog. bibliographer, bibliography

bicarb. sodium bicarbonate

b.i.d. *med.* twice a day (Latin *bis in die*)

biog. biographer, biographical, biography

biol. biological, biologist, biology

bk. (*pl.* **bks.**) bank, block., book

Bk *chem.* berkelium

bkt. basket(s), bracket

bl. bale(s), barrel(s), black, blue

b.l. or **B/L** bill of lading

bldg. building

blk. black, block, bulk

bls. bales., barrels

BLS Bureau of Labor Statistics

blvd. boulevard

b.o. back order

bor. borough.

bot. botanical, botanist, botany, bottle

br. branch, brother, bridge, brief

Br *chem.* bromine

Brit. Britain, British

bro. (*pl.* **bros.**) brother

B.S.A. Bibliographical Society of America, Boy Scouts of America

bsh. bushel

BTU, B.T.U. , b.t.u. or **btu** British thermal unit

bu. bushel(s)

bx. (*pl.* **bxs.**) box

C

C *chem.* carbon

c. about (Latin *circa*), centimeter(s), copyright, hundredweight, centigrade

C. Celsius

ca. about (Latin *circa*)

Ca *chem.* Calcium

CA California

CAB or **C.A.B.** Civil Aeronautics Board, Consumers Advisory Board

C.A.F. or **c.a.f.** cost and freight, cost, assurance and freight

cal. calendar, caliber, calorie(s)

canc. cancel, cancellation, canceled

cap. (*pl.* **caps.**) capacity, *printing* capitalize

CARE Cooperative for American Remittances Everywhere

cat. catalogue

cc. , **c.c.** or **cc** cubic centimeter(s), carbon copies

Cd *chem.* cadmium

Ce *chem.* Cerium

C.E. Chemical Engineer, Chief Engineer, Civil Engineer

CEA Council of Economic Advisers

cen. central, century

cent. centered, centigrade, centimeter(s)

cert. or **certif.** certificate

Cf *chem.* californium

cf. compare (Latin *confir*)

C.F. or **c.f.** cost and freight

C.F.I. or **c.f.i.** cost, freight, and insurance

c.f.m. or **cfm** cubic feet per minute

c.f.s. or **cfs** cubic feet per second

cg, cg. or **cgm.** centigram(s)

ch. or **Ch.** chapter

chem. chemical, chemist, chemistry

chg. (*pl.* **chgs.**) charge

chgd. charged

chm. or **chmn.** chairman

chron. or **chronol.** chronological, chronology

CIA Central Intelligence Agency

C.I.F. or **c.i.f.** cost, insurance, and freight

CIO or **C.I.O.** Congress of Industrial Organizations

circ. or **cir.** about (Latin *circa*), circular, circulation, circumference

cit. citation, cited, citizen

civ. civil., civilian

ck. (*pl.* **cks.**) cask, check

Cl *chem.* chlorine

clar. *music* clarinet

class. classic, classical, classification, classified, classify

clk. clerk, clock

C.L.U. Chartered Life Underwriter

Cm *chem.* curium

cm. or **cm** centimeter(s)

Co *chem.* cobalt

CO Colorado

c.o. or **c/o** care of

Co. or **co.** (*pl.* **cos.**)company

COBOL common business-oriented language

C.O.D. or **c.o.d.** cash on delivery, collect on delivery

C. of C. Chamber of Commerce

col. collected, collector, college, colonial, colony, color, colored, column

coll. colloquial, collect, collection, collector, college, collegiate

collat. collateral

colloq. colloquial, colloquialism, colloquially

com. commerce, commercial., common, commonly

Com. Commission, Commissioner, Committee

comb. combination, combining

coml. commercial

comm. commerce, commission, committee

comp. companion, comparative, compare, comparison, compilation, compiled, compiler, complete, composition, compositor, compound, compounded, comprising

cond. condition, *music* conducted, conductivity, conductor

conf. compare (Latin *confer*), conference

Cong. Congress, Congressional

conj. conjugation, conjunction conjunctive

cons. conserve, consigned, consignment, consolidated, consonant, construction

consol. consolidated

const. constant

constr. construction

cont. containing, contents, continue, continued, contract, contraction, contrary

contd. continued

contr. contract, contraction

contrib. contribution, contributor

CONUS Continental United States

co-op. or **coop.** cooperative

corol. or **coroll.** corollary

corp. corporation

corr. correct, corrected, correspondence, correspondent, corresponding

cp. compare

CPA or **C.P.A.** Certified Public Accountant

cr. created, credit, creditor

Cr *chem.* chromium

CR carriage return

crit. critic, criticism, criticize, critical

Cs *chem.* cesium

CST, C.S.T. or **c.s.t.** Central Standard Time

ct. cent(s), county, court, one hundred (Latin *centum*)

CT Connecticut

ctn. carton

ctr. center

cu. cubic

Cu *chem.* copper (Latin *cuprum*)

cu. cm. cubic centimeter(s)

cu. ft. cubic foot or feet

cu. in. cubic inch(es)

cur. currency, current

cu. yd. cubic yard(s)

cwt. hundredweight

cyl. cylinder, cylindrical

D

D *chem.* deuterium

d. or **D.** date, diameter, dose, *med.* give (Latin *da*)

D.A. District Attorney

dat. *gram.* dative

dau. daughter

db or **db.** decibel(s)

d. b. a. doing business as

dbl. double

DC District of Columbia

DC, D.C. or **d.c.** *electr.* direct current

dd. or **d/d** delivered

DE Delaware

deb. debenture

dec. deceased, decrease, decimeter

Dec. December

decd. deceased

decim. decimeter

decl. declension

def. defective, defendant, defense, deferred, defined, definition

deg. degree(s)

del. delegate, delete, deliver

Dem. Democrat, Democratic

demon. demonstrative

dep. departs, departure, depot, deputy

dept. department

der. derivation, derivative, derived

desc. descendant

det. detach, detachment, detail

devel. development

dia. diameter

Di *chem.* didymium

diag. diagram

dial. dialect, dialectal

diam. diameter

dict. dictionary

diff. difference, different

dim. dimension(s)

dim. or **dimin.** *music* diminuendo, diminutive

dipl. diplomat, diplomatic

dir. director

dist. distance, distant, district

dist. atty. or **Dist. Atty.** district attorney

distr. distribute, distribution, distributor

div. divided, dividend, division, divisor, divorce(d)

dlr. dealer

dlvy. delivery

doc. document

DOD Department of Defense

dom. domain, domestic, dominion

DOS disk operating system

doz. dozen(s)

Dr. Doctor, Drive

DST or **D.S.T.** or **d.s.t.** Daylight Saving Time

d.t. delirium tremens

dup. or **dupl.** duplicate

dwt. pennyweight

Dy *chem.* dysprosium

dyn. or **dynam.** dynamics

dz. dozen(s)

E

EBCDIC Extended Binary Coded Decimal Interchange Code

ECA Economic Cooperation Administration

ecol. ecological, ecology

econ. economic, economics, economy

ed. or **edit.** edited., edition., editor

EDP electronic dataprocessing

EDT or **E.D.T.** or **e.d.t.** Eastern Daylight Time

educ. education, educational

e.e. errors excepted

EEC European Economic Community

EEG *med.* electroencephalogram

EEOC Equal Employment Opportunity Commission

EFTS electronic funds transfer system

e.g. for example (Latin *exempli gratia*)

EIB or **E.I.B.** Export-Import Bank

EKG *med.* electrocardioigram

el. elevation

elec. electric, electrical, electrician

elem. element(s), elementary

elev. elevation

enc. enclosed, enclosure(s)

ency. encyclopedia

eng. or **engr.** engine, engineer, engineering, engraved, engraver, engaving

enl. enlarge(d), enlisted

env. envelope

eq. equal, equation, equator, equivalent

Er *chem.* erbium

erron. erroneous, erroneously

Es *chem.* einsteinium

ESOP employee stock option plan

esp. or **espec.** especially

ESP extrasensory perception

Esq. Esquire

est. established, estate, estimated, estuary

EST, E.S.T. or **e.s.t.** Eastern Standard Time

estab. established

ETA estimated time of arrival

et al. and others (Latin *et alii*)

Eu *chem.* europium

ex. examination, examined, example, except, excepted, exception, exchange

exam. examination, examined

exc. excellent, except, excepted, exception, exchange

exch. exchange., exchequer

excl. exclamation, exclusive

exec. executive, executor

exp. expense(s), expiration, expired, export, exported, exporter, express, experiment, experimental

ext. extension, external, externally, extinct, extra, extract

F

F *chem.* fluorine

F or **F.** fahrenheit

fac. facsimile, factor, factory

Fahr. Fahrenheit

fam. familiar, family

f.b. freight bill

FBI or **F.B.I.** Federal Bureau of Investigation

f.c. *printing* follow copy

FCC or **F.C.C.** Federal Communications Commission

FDA or **F.D.A.** Food and Drug Administration

FDIC or **F.D.I.C.** Federal Deposit Insurance Corporation

Fe *chem.* iron (Latin *ferrum*)

Feb. February

fed. federal, federated, federation

fem. feminine, female

ff *music* fortissimo

ff. folios, following

FHA Federal Housing Administration

FHLBB Federal Home Loan Bank Board

FICA Federal Insurance Contributions Act

fid. fidelity, fiduciary

FIFO first in, first out

fig. figurative(ly), figure(s)

FILO first in, last out

fl. floor, fluid, *music* flute

FL Florida

flex. flexible

fl. oz. fluid ounce(s)

Fm *chem.* fermium

FM or **F.M.** or **f.m.** frequency modulation

FMB Federal Maritime Board

FMCS Federal Mediation and Conciliation Service

F.O.B. or **f.o.b.** free on board

fol. folio, following

for. foreign, forest

FORTRAN formula translator

fpm or **f.p.m.** feet per minute

fps or **f.p.s.** feet per second

fr. fragment, from

Fr *chem.* francium

Fr. brother (Latin *Frater*), *Eccl.* Father., France, French

FRB Federal Reserve Bank, Federal Reserve Board

freq. frequency, frequent(ly)

Fri. Friday

frt. freight

FSLIC Federal Savings and Loan Insurance Corporation

ft. feet, foot, fort

FTC or **F.T.C.** Federal Trade Commission

furn. furnished, furniture

fwd. forward

G

g. or **g** gram(s)

Ga *chem.* gallium

GA Georgia

gals. gallons

GAO General Accounting Office

GATT General Agreement on Tariffs and Trade

Gd *chem.* gadolinium

gds. goods

Ge *chem.* germanium

gel. gelatinous

gen. gender, general, generally, generator, generic, genus

geog. geographer, geographic(al), geography

geol. geologist, geologic(al), geology

geom. geometric(al), geometry

ger. gerund

gloss. glossary

gm. gram(s)

G.M. general manager., Grand Master

GMT or **G.M.T.** or **G.m.t.** Greenwich mean time

GNP or **G.N.P.** gross national product

Gov. or **gov.** governor

Govt. or **govt.** government

G.P. general practitioner

GPM or **gpm** or **g.p.m.** gallons per minute

GPO or **G.P.O.** General Post Office, Government Printing Office

gr. grade, grain(s), gram(s), grammar, gross, group

gram. grammar, grammatical

gro. gross (unit of quantity)

gr. wt. grossweight

G.S.A. or **GSA** Girl Scouts of America, General Services Administration

gt. *bookbinding* gilt, great

guar. guaranteed

gym. gymnastics, gymnasium

H

H *chem.* hydrogen

hdbk. handbook

He *chem.* helium

Hf *chem.* hafnium

Hg *chem.* mercury (Latin *hydrargyrum*)

hgt. height

HI Hawaii

hist. historian, historical, history

HMO health maintenance organization

Ho *chem.* holmium

hon. honorably, honorary

Hon. Honorable

hor. horizon, horizontal

hort. horticulture, horticultural

hosp. hospital

HP or **hp**, **H.P.** or **h.p.** horsepower

ht. height

HUD Department of Housing and Urban Development

I

I *chem.* iodine

IA Iowa

ib. or **ibid.** in the same place (Latin *ibidem*)

IBT International Brotherhood of Teamsters

ICC or **I.C.C.** Interstate Commerce Commission

ICJ International Court of Justice

id. the same (Latin *idem*)

ID Idaho

I.D. or **i.d.** inside diameter

i.e. that is (Latin *id est*)

IL Illinois

illus. or **illustr.** illustrated, illustration, illustrator

IMF International Monetary Fund

imit. imitation

imp. imperative, imperfect, imperial, import, imported, importer., important

IN Indiana

in. inch(es)

In *chem.* indium

inc. inclosure, including, inclusive, income, incorporated, increase

incl. inclosure, including, inclusive

incog. incognito

incr. increased, increasing

ind. independent, index, indicated, indicative, indirect, industrial

indef. indefinite

indent. *printing* indention

indic. indicating, indicative, indicator

inf. below (Latin *infra*), inferior, infinitive, information

init. initial, in the beginning (Latin *initio*)

ins. inches, inspector, insular, insulated, insulation, insurance

insol. insoluble

insp. inspected, inspector

inst. instant, instantaneous, instrument(al)

Inst. Institute, Institution

instr. instruction, instrument(al)

int. intelligence, interest, interior, interjection, internal, international, interval, intransitive

inter. intermediate

interrog. interrogative

intr. intransitive

intro. introduction, introductory

inv. invented, invention, inventor, invoice

Io *chem.* ionium

i.q. the same as (Latin *idem quod*)

IQ or **I.Q.** intelligence quotient

Ir *chem.* iridium

irreg. irregular(ly)

IRS Internal Revenue Service

it. or **ital.** italic(s)

J

Jan. January

jct. or **jctn.** junction

jour. journal, journeyman

J.P. Justice of the Peace

Jr. or **jr.** junior

Jul. July

jun. junior

Jun. June

junc. junction

K

K *chem.* potassium

K or **k** kilo

KB or **Kb** kilobyte

kc. or **kc** kilocycle(s)

kg. or **kg** kilograms

km. or **km** kilometer(s)

Kr *chem.* krypton

KS Kansas

kv. or **kv** kilovolt(s)

kw. or **kw** kilowatt(s)

K.W.H., kwh, kilowatt hour(s)

KY Kentucky

L

l. or **l** liter

La *chem.* lanthanum

LA Louisiana

lab. laboratory

LAN local area network

lang. language

lat. latitude

LBO leveraged buyout

lb(s). pound(s) (Latin *libra, librae*)

l.c. in the place cited (Latin *lococitato*), *printing* lower case

L/C or **l/c** letter of credit

L.C.L. or **l.c.l.** less than carload lot

lect. lecture, lecturer

LED light-emitting diode

legis. legislation, legislature

lex. lexicon

l.f. or **lf** *printing* lightface

lg. or **lge.** large

Li *chem.* lithium

lib. book (Latin *liber*), librarian, library

LILO last in, last out

LIFO last in, first out

lin. lineal., linear

ling. linguistics

liq. liquid., liquor

lit. liter, literal(ly), literary, literature

lith., litho. or **lithog.** lithograph, lithography

ll. lines

loc. cit. in the place cited (Latin *loco citato*)

long. longitude

Lr *chem.* lawrencium

ltd. or **Ltd.** limited

Lu *chem.* lutetium

M

m or **m.** meter(s)

Ma *chem.* masurium

MA Massachusetts

mach. machine, machinery, machinist

MADD Mothers Against Drunk Driving

mag. magazine, magnet, magnetism

manuf. manufacture(d), manufacturer, manufacturing

Mar. March

marg. margin, margina

mas. or **masc.** masculine

math. mathematical, mathematician, mathematics

max. maximum

mc or **m.c.** or **mc.** megacycle

M.C. Master of Ceremonies

Md *chem.* mendelevium

MD Maryland

M.D. Doctor of Medicine (Latin *MedicinaeDoctor*)

mdse. merchandise

ME Maine

ME, ME. or **M.E.** Middle English

meas. measure

mech. mechanical, mechanics, mechanism

med. medical, medicine, medium

mem. member, memoir, memorandum, memorial

memo. memorandum

mf or **mf.** *music* moderately loud (Ital. *mezzo forte*)

mfg. manufacturing

mfr. manufacture, manufacturer

mg., mg or **mgm** milligram(s)

Mg *chem.* magnesium

mgr. manager

MI Michigan

mi. mile(s)

min. mineralogical, mineralogy, minimum, minute(s)

misc. miscellaneous, miscellany

mk. mark(s)

mkt. market

ml. milliliter(s)

mm. or **mm** millimeter(s)

m.m. with the necessary changes (Latin *mutatis mutandis*)

Mn *chem.* manganese

MN Minnesota

mo. (*pl.* **mos.**) month(s)

Mo *chem.* molybdenum

MO Missouri

mod. moderate, *music* moderato, modern

Mon. Monday

m.p.h. or **mph** miles per hour

MS Mississippi

MS., MS, ms. or **ms** manuscript

msg. message

MSG monosodium glutamate

MSS. MSS, mss. or **mss** manuscripts

MST, M.S.T. or **m.s.t.** mountain standard time

Mt. or **mt.** (*pl.* **mts.**)mount, mountain

MT Montana

mtg. meeting

mtge. mortgage

mtn. mountain

mus. museum, music, musician

myth. or **mythol.** mythology

N

N *chem.* nitrogen

Na *chem.* sodium (Latin *natrium*)

NAACP or **N.A.A.C.P.** National Association for the Advancement of Colored People

NAM National Association of Manufacturers

NASA National Aeronautics and Space Administration

natl. national

NATO North Atlantic Treaty Organization

Nb *chem.* niobium

N.B. or **n.b.** note well (Latin *nota bene*)

NBS or **N.B.S.** National Bureau of Standards

NC North Carolina

NCAA or **N.C.A.A.** National Collegiate Athletic Association

Nd *chem.* neodymium

ND North Dakota

Ne *chem.* neon

NE Nebraska

NEA National Education Association

neg. negative

neut. neuter

N.G. or **n.g.** no good

NH New Hampshire

Ni *chem.* nickel

NJ New Jersey

NLRB or **N.L.R.B.** National Labor Relations Board

NM New Mexico

No *Chem.* nobelium

No. or **no.** north, northern, number

nom. nominative

Nos. or **nos.** numbers

NOW National Organization for Women

Nov. November

Np *Chem.* neptunium

N.P. Notary Public

nr. near

NRC National Research Council, Nuclear Regulatory Commission

N.S.F. or **N/S/F** not sufficient funds

N.S.P.C.A. National Society for the Prevention of Cruelty to Animals

Nt *chem.* niton

NTSB National Transportation Safety Board

nt. wt. net weight

num. numeral(s)

NV Nevada

NY New York

NYSE New York Stock Exchange

O

O *chem.* oxygen

OAS Organization of American States

obit. obituary

obj. object, objection, objective

obs. observation, obsolete

o.c. in the work cited (Latin *opere citato*)

OCR optical character recognition, optical character reading

Oct. October

O.D., OD or **o.d.** outside diameter, overdraft, overdrawn

OEEC or **O.E.E.C.** Organization for European Economic Cooperation

off. offered, office, officer, official

OH Ohio

OK Oklahoma

OMB Office of Management and Budget

op. cit. in the work cited (Latin *opere citato*)

OPEC Organization of Petroleum Exporting Countries

opp. opposed, opposite

ord. ordained, order, ordinal, ordinance, ordinary

OR Oregon

org. organic, organized

OSHA Occupational Safety and Health Administration

orig. original(ly)

Os *chem.* osmium

oz. (*pl.* **ozs.**) ounce

P

P *chem.* phosphorus

p.a. yearly (Latin *per annum*)

Pa *chem.* protactinium

PA Pennsylvania

PA press agent, public address system

P.A. or **P/A** power of attorney, purchasing agent

par. paragraph, parallel, parenthesis

part. participle, particular

pass. passage, passenger, passive

pat. patent(ed), pattern

patd. patented

Pat. Off. Patent Office

payt. payment

Pb *chem.* lead (Latin *plumbum*)

PBS Public Broadcasting Service

pc. (*pl.* **pcs.**) piece, price

P/C or **p/c** petty cash

PC personal computer

pct. percent

pd. paid

Pd *chem.* palladium

Pen. or **pen.** peninsula

per. period, person

perf. perfect, perforated

perm. permanent

pert. pertaining

Phar., phar., Pharm. or **pharm.** pharmaceutical, pharmacy

phil. philosopher, philosophical, philosophy

phon. phonetics

phot. photograph, photographic, photography

phr. phrase

PHS Public Health Service

phys. physical, physician, physicist, physics

pk. (*pl.* **pks.**) pack, park, peak, peck

pkg. package(s)

pkt. packet

pl. place, plural

plat. plateau

plu. plural

plur. plural, plurality

Pm *chem.* promethium

P.M. or **p.m.** afternoon (Latin *post meridiem*)

P.M. or **PM** Postmaster

Po *chem.* polonium

P.O. or **p.o.** postal order, post office

pop. popular, popularly, population

POP point of purchase

pos. positive, possessive

poss. possession, possessive, possible, possibly

pp. pages, *music* pianissimo

P.P. or **p.p.** parcel post, postpaid

p.p. parcel post, past participle

ppd. postpaid, prepaid

ppl. participial

p.p.m. or **ppm.** or **ppm** parts per million

ppr. or **p.pr.** present participle

P.P.S. or **p.p.s.** additional postscript (Latin *post postscriptum*)

pr. pair(s), paper, present, price, printing, pronoun

Pr *chem.* praseodymium

PR Puerto Rico, public relations

prec. preceding

pred. predicate

pref. preface, prefatory, preference, prefix

pres. present

Pres. President

pret. preterit

prim. primary, primitive

print. printing

prod. produce(d), product

Prof. or **prof.** professor

prog. progressive

prop. proper(ly), property, proposition, proprietor, proprietary

prov. province, provincial, provisional

prs. pairs

P.S. or **p.s.** postscript

p.s.f. or **psf** pounds per square foot

p.s.i. or **psi** pounds per square inch

PST, P.S.T. or **p.s.t.** Pacific Standard Time

psychol. psychological, psychologist, psychology

pt. part, pint(s), point(s)

Pt *chem.* platinum

PTA or **P.T.A.** Parent-Teacher Association

ptg. printing

pts. parts, pints, points

Pu *chem.* plutonium

pub. public, publication, published, publisher, publishing

pwt. pennyweight

Q

Q.E.D. Which was to be demonstrated (Latin *quod erat demonstrandum*)

qq.v. which see (Latin *quae vide*)

qt. quantity, quart(s)

ques. question

q.v. which see (Latin *quae vide*)

R

r. radius, rare, right-hand page (Latin *recto*)

Ra *chem.* radium

RAM random-access memory

Rb *chem.* rubidium

rcd. received

rd. road, rod(s), round

R.D. Rural Delivery

Re *chem.* rhenium

REA Rural Electrification Administration

rec. receipt, received, recipe, record, recorded, recorder, recording

recit. recitative

rec. sec. recording secretary

ref. reference, referred, refund

refl. reflection, reflective(ly), reflex, reflexive

reg. region, register(ed), regular(ly), Regulation

REIT real estate investment trust

rel. relating, relative(ly), released

rep. report, representative

repr. reprinted

req. required, request, requisition

res. research, residence, reserve, resides

resp. respective(ly), respondent

retd. retained, returned

rev. revenue, reverse(d), review(ed), revise(d), revision, revolution

RFD or **R.F.D.** Rural Free Delivery

r.h. relative humidity, right hand

Rh *chem.* rhodium

rhet. rhetoric(al)

RI Rhode Island

R.I.P. rest in peace(Latin *requiescat* or *requiescant in pace*)

RISC reduced instruction set computer

rm. (*pl.* **rms.**) ream, room

Rn *chem.* radon

RNA *biochem.* ribonucleic acid

rom. *printing* Roman (type)

ROM read-only memory

rpm or **r.p.m.** revolutions per minute

rps or **r.p.s.** revolutions per second

rpt. report

RR or **R.R.** railroad, rural route

R.S.V.P. or **r.s.v.p.** please reply (French *Répondez s'il vous plaît*)

rt. right

Ru *chem.* ruthenium

S

S *chem.* sulfur

Sa *chem.* samarium

Sat. Saturday, Saturn

SAT Scholastic Aptitude Test

sb. substantive

Sb *chem.* antimony (Latin *stibium*)

s.c. *printing* small capitals, super-calendered

Sc *chem.* scandium

SC South Carolina

s. caps *printing* small capitals

sci. science, scientific

SD South Dakota

Se *chem.* selenium

sec. according to (Latin *secundum*), secant, second(s), secondary, secretary, section(s), sector

SEC or **S.E.C.** Securities and Exchange Commission.

sect. section, sectional

secty. secretary

Sen. or **sen.** senate, senator, senior

sep. separate

Sep. or **Sept.** September

seq. sequel, sequence

ser. serial, series

sgd. signed

shpt. shipment

Si *chem.* silicon

sig. signature

sing. singular

Sm *chem.* samarium

Sn *chem.* tin (Latin *stannum*)

soc. social, society

sol. soluble, solution

sop. *music* soprano

sp. special, species, specific, specimen, spelling

sq. square

Sr *chem.* strontium

SRO or **S.R.O.** standing room only

st. street

sta. station, stationary

std. standard

ster. or **stg.** sterling

stge. storage

stk. stock

str. steamer, strait

sub. subscription, substitute, suburb, suburban

subj. subject, subjective(ly), subjunctive

subst. substantive, substitute

suf. or **suff.** suffix

Sun. Sunday

sup. above (Latin *supra*), superior, superlative, supplement, supplementary, supply

super. superintendent, superior

superl. superlative

supp. or **suppl.** supplement, supplementary

supr. supreme

supt. superintendent

sur. surcharge, surplus

surg. surgeon, surgery, surgical

surv. survey, surveying, surveyor, surviving

syl. or **syll.** syllable, syllabus

sym. symbol, symphony, symptom

syn. synonym

synop. synopsis

syst. system, systematic

T

t. teaspoon

T *chem.* tantalum

T. tablespoon

Ta *chem.* tantalum

tab. table(s), tabulate, tabulation

Tb *chem.* terbium

t.b. trial balance

tbs. or **tbsp.** tablespoon(s)

Tc *chem.* technetium

Te *chem.* tellurium

technol. technology

tel. telegram, telegraph, telegraphic, telephone

temp. temperature, temporary

ter. terrace, territorial, territory

term. terminal, termination, terminology

Th *chem.* thorium

Thur. Thursday

Ti *chem.* titanium

Tl *chem.* thallium

Tm *chem.* thulium

TN Tennessee

tng. training

top. topographical, topography

tp. township

tr. trace, train, transitive, translated, translation, translator, transpose

Tr *chem.* terbium

trans. transaction(s), transferred, *gram.* transitive, translated, translation, translator, transportation, transpose, transverse

transl. translated, translation

transp. transparent, transportation

treas. treasurer, treasury

trfd. transferred

tripl. triplicate

Tues. Tuesday

TVA or **T.V.A.** Tennessee Valley Authority

twp. township

TX Texas

typ. or **typog.** typographic(al), typography

U

U *chem.* uranium

UAW or **U.A.W.** United Automobile Workers

u.c. *music* soft pedal (Ital. *una corda,* one string), *printing* uppercase

UFO unidentified flying object

ult. ultimate(ly)

UN or **U.N.** United Nations

UNEF United Nations Emergency Force

UNESCO or **Unesco** The United Nations Educational, Scientific and Cultural Organization

UNICEF or **Unicef** United Nations Children's Fund

univ. universal(ly), university

unpub. unpublished

Ur *chem.* uranium

US or **U.S.** United States

USA or **U.S.A.** United States of America

U.S.C. & G.S. United States Coast and Geodetic Survey

USCG or **U.S.C.G.** United States Coast Guard

USDA United States Department of Agriculture

USIA or **U.S.I.A.** United States Information Agency

USPHS or **U.S.P.H.S.** United States Public Health Service

USPS United States Postal Service

USS or **U.S.S.** United States Ship (or Steamer or Steamship)

UT Utah

V

v. *gram.* verb, vocative, verse, version, versus, volt, voltage, volume

V *chem.* vanadium

VA Virginia

var. variant, variation, variety

VAT value added tax

v. aux. *gram.* auxiliary verb

vb. verb, verbal

Vd *chem.* vanadium

VDT video display terminal

ver. verse(s), version

VHF, vhf, V.H.F., or **v.h.f.** very high frequency

v.i. *gram.* intransitive verb

Vi *chem.* virginium

VI Virgin Islands

vil. village

VIP or **V.I.P.** very important person

VISTA Volunteers in Service to America

viz. namely (Latin *videlicet*)

vocab. vocabulary

vol. volume, volunteer

vols. volumes

vs. verse, versus
VSS versions
v.t. *gram.* transitive verb
VT Vermont
v.v. viceversa

W

W *chem.* tungsten (Latin *wolfram*)
WA Washington
W.b. , W/b, W.B. or W/B waybill
Wed. Wednesday
wf or w.f. *printing* wrong font
WHO World Health Organization
WI Wisconsin
wk. (*pl.* wks.) week, work
wkly. weekly
wt. weight
WV West Virginia
WY Wyoming

X

x-cp. , X.C. or x.c. Ex coupon
x-div. , X.D. or x.d. Ex dividend
Xe *chem.* xenon
x-ref. cross-reference

Y

Y *chem.* yttrium
Yb *chem.* ytterbium
yd. (*pl.* yds.) yard
yr. year, your
yrs. years, yours
Yt *chem.* yttrium

Z

Z. or z. zone
Zn *chem.* zinc
zool. zoological, zoologist, zoology
Zr *chem.* zirconium

FORMS OF ADDRESS

President of the United States

Address: Business: The President
The White House
Washington, D.C.

Social: The President and Mrs. ____ (*Last name*)
The White House
Washington, D.C.

Salutation: Formal: Mr. President:
Informal: Dear Mr. President:

Closing: Formal: Most respectfully yours,
Informal: Sincerely yours,

In conversation: Mr. President *or* Sir

Title of introduction: The President *or* Mr. ____ (*Last name*)

Vice President of the United States

Address:Business: The Vice President
United States Senate
Washington, D.C.

Social: The Vice President and Mrs. ____ (*Last name*)
Home address

Salutation:Formal: Mr. Vice President:
Informal: Dear Mr. Vice President:

Closing: Formal: Very truly yours,
Informal: Sincerely yours,

In conversation: Mr. Vice President *or* Sir

Title of introduction: The Vice President *or* Mr. ____ (*Last name*)

Chief Justice of the United States

Address:Business: The Chief Justice
The Supreme Court
Washington, D.C.

      Social: The Chief Justice
or The Chief Justice and
Mrs. *or* Mr. ____ (*Last name*)
Home address

Salutation:Formal: Sir:
      Informal: Dear Mr. *or* Ms. Chief Justice:

Closing: Formal: Very truly yours,
      Informal: Sincerely yours,

In conversation: Mr. *or* Ms. Chief Justice; Sir *or* Madame

Title of introduction: The Chief Justice

Associate Justice of the Supreme Court

Address:Business: Mr. Justice *or* Madam Justice ____ (*Last name*)
The Supreme Court
Washington, D.C.

      Social: Mr. Justice *or* Madam Justice ____ (*Full name*);
or Mr. Justice *or* Madam Justice and
Mrs. *or* Mr. ____ (*Last name*)
Home address

Salutation:Formal: Sir: *or* Madam:
      Informal: Dear Mr. Justice:
or Madam Justice ____ (*Last name*):

Closing: Formal: Very sincerely yours,
      Informal: Sincerely yours,

In conversation: Mr. Justice *or* Madam Justice;
Mr. Justice *or* Madam Justice ____ (*Last name*);
Sir *or* Madam

Title of introduction: Mr. Justice *or* Madam Justice ____ (*Last name*)

Reference

Cabinet Officer

Address:Business: The Honorable ____ (*Full name*)
Secretary of the Treasury,
Attorney General of the United States, etc.
Washington, D.C.

Social: The Honorable ____ (*Full name*);
or The Secretary of the Treasury
and Mrs. *or* Mr. ____ (*Last name*)
Home address

Salutation:Formal: Sir: *or* Dear Sir: *or* Madam:
Informal: Dear Mr. Secretary: *or* Dear Madam Secretary:

Closing: Formal: Very truly yours,
Informal: Sincerely yours,

In conversation: Mr. Secretary *or* Madam Secretary;
Mr. Attorney General;
Mr. *or* Ms. ____ (*Last name*)

Title of introduction: The Secretary of the Treasury,
Mr. ____ (*Last name*)
or The Secretary of the Treasury,
Ms. ____ (*Last name*)

Former President

Address:Business: The Honorable ____ (*Full name*)
Office address

Social: The Honorable ____ (*Full name*)
or The Honorable and Mrs. ____ (*Full name*)
Home address

Salutation:Formal: Sir:
Informal: Dear Mr. ____ (*Last name*):

Closing: Formal: Very truly yours,
Informal: Sincerely yours,

In conversation: Mr. ____ (*Last name*)*or* Sir

Title of introduction: The Honorable ____ (*Full name*)

United States Senator

Address:Business: The Honorable ____ (*Full name*)
United States Senate
Washington, D.C.

Social: The Honorable (*Full name*);
or The Honorable and Mrs. *or* Mr. ____(*Full name*)
Home address

Salutation:Formal: Sir: *or* Madam:
Informal: Dear Senator ____ (*Last name*):

Closing: Formal: Very truly yours,
Informal: Sincerely yours,

In conversation: Senator; *or* Senator ____ (*Last name*);
or Sir *or* Madam

Title of introduction: Senator ____ (*Last name*)

Speaker of the House of Representatives

Address:Business: The Honorable ____ (*Full name*)
The Speaker of the House of Representatives
Washington, D.C.

Social: The Speaker of the House of Representatives
and Mrs. *or* Mr. ____ (*Last name*)
Home address

Salutation:Formal: Sir: *or* Madam:
Informal: Dear Mr. *or* Madam Speaker:

Closing: Formal: Very truly yours,
Informal: Sincerely yours,

In conversation: Mr. *or* Madam Speaker; Sir *or* Madam

Title of introduction: The Speaker of the House of Representatives;
The Speaker, Mr. *or* Ms. ____ (*Last name*)

Reference

Member of the House of Representatives

Address: Business: The Honorable _____ (*Full name*)
United States House of Representatives
Washington, D.C.

Social: The Honorable _____ (*Full name*);
or The Honorable and Mrs. *or* Mr. _____ (*Full name*)
Home address

Salutation: Formal: Sir: *or* Madam:
Informal: Dear Mr. *or* Ms. _____ (*Last name*):

Closing: Formal: Very truly yours,
Informal: Sincerely yours,

In conversation: Mr. or Ms. _____ (*Last name*); Sir *or* Madam

Title of introduction: Representative _____ (*Last name*)

Ambassador of the United States

Address: Business: The Honorable _____ (*Full name*)
The Ambassador of the United States
American Embassy
(*City, Country*)

Social: The Honorable _____ (*Full name*);
or The Honorable and Mrs. *or* Mr. _____ (*Full name*)
Home address

Salutation: Formal: Sir: *or* Madam:
Informal: Dear Mr. *or* Madam Ambassador:

Closing: Formal: Very truly yours,
Informal: Sincerely yours,

In conversation: Mr. *or* Madam Ambassador; Sir *or* Madam

Title of introduction: The American Ambassador
or The Ambassador of the United States

Minister Plenipotentiary of the United States

Address: Business: The Honorable ___ (*Full name*)
The Minister of the United States
American Legation
(*City, Country*)

Social: The Honorable ___ (*Full name*);
or The Honorable and Mr. or Mrs. ___ (*Full name*)
Home address

Salutation: Formal: Sir: or Madam:
Informal: Dear Mr. or Madam Minister:

Closing: Formal: Very truly yours,
Informal: Sincerely yours,

In conversation: Mr. or Ms. ___ (*Last name*)

Title of introduction: Mr. or Ms. ___ (*Last name*), the American
Minister

Consul of the United States

Address: Business: Mr. or Ms. ___ (*Full name*)
American Consul
(*City, Country*)

Social: Mr. and Mrs. (*Full name*)
Home address

Salutation: Formal: Sir: or Madam: or Dear Sir: or Madam:
Informal: Dear Mr. or Ms. ___ (*Last name*):

Closing: Formal: Very truly yours,
Informal: Sincerely yours,

In conversation: Mr. or Ms. ___ (*Last name*)

Title of introduction: Mr. or Ms. ___ (*Last name*)

Reference

Ambassador of a foreign country

Address:Business: The Honorable ____ (*Full name*)
The Minister-of ____ (*Country*)
Washington, D.C.

Social: The Honorable and Mrs. *or* Mr. ____ (*Last name*)
Home address

Salutation:Formal: Sir: *or* Madam:
Informal: Dear Mr. *or* Madam Minister:

Closing: Formal: Very truly yours,
Informal: Sincerely yours,

In conversation: Mr. *or* Madam Minister; Sir *or* Madam

Title of introduction: The Minister of ____ (*Country*)

Governor of a State

Address:Business: The Honorable ____ (*Full name*)
Governor of (State)
(*Capital city, State*)

Social: The Honorable ____ (*Full name*);
or The Honorable and Mrs. *or* Mr. ____ (*Full name*)
Home address

Salutation:Formal: Sir: *or* Madam:
Informal: Dear Governor ____ (*Last name*):

Closing: Formal: Very truly yours,
Informal: Sincerely yours,

In conversation: Governor ____ (*Last name*) *or* Sir *or* Madam

Title of introduction: The Governor *or* The Governor of ____ (*State*)

State Senators and Representatives

Address in the same manner as U.S. Senators and Representatives

Grammar Handbook

Mayor

Address: Business: Honorable ____ (*Full name*)
Mayor of ____ (*City*)
City Hall
(*City, State*)

Social: The Honorable ____ (*Full name*)
or The Honorable and Mrs. *or* Mr. ____ (*Full name*)
Home address

Salutation: Formal: Sir: *or* Madam:
Informal: Dear Mayor ____ (*Last name*):

Closing: Formal: Very truly yours,
Informal: Sincerely yours,

In conversation: Mr. Mayor *or* Madam Mayor

Title of introduction: Mayor ____ (*Last name*)

Protestant Bishop

Address: Business: The Right Reverend ____ (*Full name*)
Bishop of ____
(*City, State*)

Social: The Right Reverend and Mrs. ____ (*Full name*)
Home address

Salutation: Formal: Right Reverend Sir:
Informal: Dear Bishop Bowman:

Closing: Formal: Respectfully yours,
Informal: Sincerely yours,

In conversation: Bishop ____ (*Last name*)

Title of introduction: Bishop ____ (*Last name*)

226

Reference

Protestant Clergyman

Address:Business: The Reverend ____ (*Full name,*
followed by degree, if any)
Church address

Social: The Reverend *or* Dr. and Mrs. *or* Mr. (*Full name*);
or (*if husband and wife are both clergy*)
The Reverend Mr. and Mrs. ____ (*Last name*)
Home address

Salutation:Formal: Dear Sir *or* Madam:
Informal: Dear Mr. *or* Ms. *or* Dr. ____ (*Last name*):

Closing: Formal: Sincerely yours,
Informal: Sincerely yours,

In conversation: Mr. *or* Mrs. *or* Dr. ____ (*Last name*)

Title of introduction: Mr. *or* Mrs. *or* Dr. ____ (*Last name*)

Rabbi

Address:Business: Rabbi ____ (*Full name, followed by degree, if any*)
Synagogue address

Social: Rabbi *or* Dr. and Mrs. *or* Mr. ____ (*Full name*);
or (if husband and wife are both rabbis)
The Rabbis Mr. and Mrs. ____ (*Last name*)
Home address

Salutation:Formal: Dear Sir *or* Madam:
Informal: Dear Rabbi *or* Doctor:

Closing: Formal: Sincerely yours,
Informal: Sincerely yours,

In conversation: Rabbi *or* Dr. ____ (*Last name*)

Title of introduction: Rabbi *or* Dr. ____ (*Last name*)

The Pope

Address: His Holiness Pope Paul VI
or His Holiness the Pope
Vatican City

Salutation: Your Holiness:

Closing: Your Holiness' most humble servant,

In conversation: Your Holiness

Title of introduction: *One is presented to:* His Holiness
or The Holy Father

Cardinal

Address: His Eminence (*First name*) Cardinal (*Last name*)
Archbishop of ____
(*City, State*)

Salutation:Formal: Your Eminence:
Informal: Dear Cardinal (*Last name*):

Closing: Your Eminence's humble servant,

In conversation: Your Eminence

Title of introduction: *One is presented to:*
His Eminence Cardinal ____ (*Last name*)

Roman Catholic Archbishop

Address: The Most Reverend ____ (*Full name*)
Archbishop of ____
(*City, State*)

Salutation:Formal: Your Excellency: *or* Most Reverend Sir:
Informal: Dear Archbishop (*Last name*):

Closing: Your Escellency's humble servant,

In conversation: Your Excellency

Title of introduction: *One is presented to:*
The Most Reverend ____ (*Last name*)
The Archbishop of ____

Reference

Roman Catholic Bishop

Address: The Most Reverend ____ (*Full name*)
Church address

Salutation: Formal: Your Excellency: *or* Most Reverend Sir:
Informal: Dear Bishop ____ (*Last name*):

Closing: Formal: Your obedient servant,
Informal: Sincerely yours,

In conversation: Your Excellency

Title of introduction: Bishop ____ (*Last name*)

Monsignor

Address: The Right Reverend Monsignor ____ (*Last name*)
Church address

Salutation: Formal: Right Reverend Monsignor:
Informal: Dear Monsignor Ryan:

Closing: Formal: I remain, Right Reverend Monsignor,
yours faithfully,
Informal: Faithfully yours,

In conversation: Monsignor ____ (*Last name*)

Title of introduction: Monsignor ____ (*Last name*)

Priest

Address: The Reverend ____ (*Full name,
and the initials of his order*)
Church address

Salutation: Formal: Reverend Father:
Informal: Dear Father ____ (*Last name*):

Closing: Formal: I remain, Reverend Father,
yours faithfully,
Informal: Faithfully yours,

In conversation: Father *or* Father ____ (*Last name*)

Title of introduction: The Reverend Father ____ (*Last name*)

Member of a Religious Order

Address: Sister *or* Brother ____ (*Full name, and initials of the order*)
Home address

Salutation: Formal: Dear Sister: *or* Brother:
Informal: Dear Sister *or* Brother ____ (*First name*):

Closing: Formal: Respectfully yours,
Informal: Faithfully yours,

In conversation: Sister *or* Brother ____ (*First name*)
Title of introduction: Sister *or* Brother ____ (*First name*)

University Professor

Address: Business: Professor ____ (*Full name*)
Office address

Social: Professor *or* Dr. and Mrs. *or* Mr. ____ (*Full name*)
Home address

Salutation: Formal: Dear Professor *or* Dr. ____ (*Last name*):
Informal: Dear Mr. *or* Ms. ____ (*Last name*):

Closing: Formal: Very truly yours,
Informal: Sincerely yours,

In conversation: Professor *or* Dr. *or* Mr. *or* Ms. ____ (*Last name*)
Title of introduction: Professor *or* Dr. ____ (*Last name*)

Physician

Address: Business: ____ (*Full name*), M.D. *or* Dr. ____ (*Full name*)
Office address

Social: Dr. and Mrs. *or* Mr. ____ (*Full name*)
Home address

Salutation: Dear Dr. ____ (*Last name*):

Closing: Formal: Very truly yours,
Informal: Sincerely yours,

In conversation: Dr. ____ (*Last name*)
Title of Introduction: Dr. ____ (*Last name*)

Index

Index

Index

Index

Reference lists

On the theory that we learn by example, this book is sprinkled liberally with word lists and examples. Following is a list of the lists